MW01631781

THE WINNING EDGE

THE WINNING EDGE

BROOKS JOHNSON

ATHENEUM
NEW YORK 1988

ACKNOWLEDGEMENTS

I would like to acknowledge the many athletes from whom I've learned so very much and three coaches who have helped to shape my ideas on coaching: Carlo Guidaboni, Ding Dussalt, and Ted Hayden.

Atheneum
Macmillan Publishing Company
866 Third Avenue, New York, N.Y. 10022
Collier Macmillan Canada, Inc.

Library of Congress Cataloging-in-Publication Data
Johnson, Brooks———
The winning edge.
1. Running. 2. Running—Training. 3. Running races.
I. Title.
GV1061. J55 1988 796.4'26 88-6348
ISBN 0-689-11555-5

Macmillan books are available at special discounts for bulk purchases for sales promotions, premiums, fund-raising, or educational use. For details, contact:

Special Sales Director
Macmillan Publishing Company
866 Third Avenue
New York, N.Y. 10022

10 9 8 7 6 5 4 3 2 1

Printed in the United States of America

For my mother,
Dorothy Fontes
and my wife,
Deeane Johnson

CONTENTS

INTRODUCTION

All of us have admired and envied those people around us who "have it." These people go through life always a step up on everyone else. They have that "little bit extra" that allows them to succeed when others fail. They are the ones with a permanent rabbit's foot. They have what I call the "Winning Edge."

In running, the Winning Edge is not one thing but actually many things that vary from person to person and sometimes from race to race. It can be generally divided into two basic areas: psychological and physical.

In too many instances, we assume that if we have not been successful to date, or as successful as we would like to be, then we probably do not possess the Winning Edge. We further assume that we do not have much of a chance of ever acquiring it. But in fact, not having the Winning Edge and not getting it are two quite different things.

We see the winners in life appearing so "natural" in their victories that we think they were simply born advantaged. The truth is that things that make the difference between winners and losers are things that most of us can identify, develop, and exploit. Regardless of a person's basic gifts, success and winning are learned experiences. Some people appear to learn faster, and, perhaps, even more easily than others, but most of us can learn to be more successful and ultimately to become winners.

During my more than thirty years of in-depth involvement in athletics—first as an athlete and later as a coach—I have had excellent opportunities to observe and experience the ingredients that go into developing the Winning Edge. My experience in track and field ranges from the various age-group levels through the Olympic Games, and my exposure to the Winning Edge has been broad and intimate.

I, too, began life thinking that some people are just "naturals" and that because I was not a natural, there was not much I could do about becoming one. But I soon learned that nothing is further from the truth. All winning habits, movements, and attitudes can be learned—everyone has at least the potential to improve if he finds out what is required and then practices with all his heart.

Although I have since heard myself mistakenly described as a natural athlete, the victories I have enjoyed did not come easily. My successes came only after a tough regimen and hard training; they were agonizing experiences for me because I was not, in reality, a natural. When people later assumed certain things had not been difficult for me, I got angry: I knew firsthand all the work that went into those seemingly easy wins.

I first developed a healthy disregard for assumptions about natural talents at my Plymouth, Massachusetts, high school. It was at my senior prom and I remember how embarrassed I felt. I was one of the four class officers, and each of us had been asked to dance with a parent. My high school was virtually all white, and my mother and I were the only two blacks at the prom. My trauma centered around the fact that despite being black, my mother did not, as is generally assumed even today, have "natural rhythm." While the band, myself, and everyone else were accenting the second and fourth beats, my mother accented the first and third. When I was beeping, she was bopping. Being the only black couple on the floor, we were the focus of everyone as we pointed and counterpointed around the room.

The upshot of this mortifying experience for me was to forever suspect those things that some people are supposed to possess naturally. My reluctance to accept these kinds of myths and stereotypes has helped me in many ways over the years—to get the best out of myself and the athletes I have coached. Having a healthy suspicion about what is considered "commonly known" and natural about running is probably the best attitude to have when you are seeking to improve.

Let me give another example. One of the biggest myths and stereotypes in running today is the idea that blacks are naturally faster than whites, but neither anatomy nor statistics support this false notion. If you look at the Olympic Games—which represent the broadest spectrum of athletes—you find that from 1948 through 1984 there have been exactly five white and five black male Olympic 100-meter sprint champions. Interestingly enough, in that time only three 100-meter gold medalists have doubled to win the 200 meter as well. Of these three, two were white, and until Carl Lewis did it in 1984, no other black runner had accomplished it since 1936!

White athletes won the Olympic 100 meters from 1952 to 1960, a time spanning three Olympiads. To date, black runners have not achieved three consecutive Olympic sprint victories. So if one were looking for racial superiority in Olympic 100-meter sprints, then the edge should probably go to the white sprinters. Yet this, too, is a meaningless assumption.

The fallacy that blacks naturally have the Winning Edge in sprinting clearly illustrates the first principle of my athletic and coaching career: Progress is rarely made by accepting what is commonly accepted. You cannot gain a Winning Edge if you simply rely on conventions. Progress usually comes only when you find an "uncommon" way—a new way, a different way—to understand and apply basic principles. To gain a Winning Edge, you must learn where myth ends and science and application begin. You must learn what aspects of a situation are important to your effort and find a unique way to exploit them to positive advantage.

This book, then, is written for the runner who is willing to accept the challenge of creating an opportunity to improve his or her speed, technique, and safety, as well as enjoyment—to develop the Winning Edge. What is shared here are insights, ideas, experiences, and information that will provide the reader with a basis from which he or she can get more out of running. However, please note that the Basic Training Program set forth in Chapter 5 assumes a certain fitness level which may exceed that of the recreational jogger: he or she should consult a physician before undertaking this strenuous physical activity.

By taking relevant points made here and applying them intelligently, running improvement is virtually assured. In the pages that follow, I cover the spectrum of needs and deficiencies of recreational joggers, weekend racers (whom I refer to as weekend warriors), and world-class athletes alike. Since the basis of what is said here comes from my experience with all types of runners, the points have broad application. If you want to run more efficiently, more competitively, and with greater satisfaction, you will find something valuable here for you.

1

THE WINNING EDGE

What is this phenomenon I call the Winning Edge?

In 1948, Harrison Dillard was considered the number one hurdler in the world. At the Olympic trials in Evanston, Illinois, he hit a hurdle and did not qualify for the U.S. team in his best event. In those days, the selection of the U.S. team was not as structured as it is now, so despite the fact Dillard did not make the team in the hurdles, he was able to gain a berth on the team in the 100-meter dash. At the Olympics in London later that year he ran off with the gold medal—in what was not supposed to be his event.

Even though Dillard had suffered a crushing defeat in his specialty, he got back up, got his head together, and made the most of his new opportunity. He refused to let himself become distraught and distracted, and instead found another way of using his talents. Clearly, he had the Winning Edge.

Ed Temple, the coach at Tennessee State University who has coached more Olympic medalists than anyone else in the world, credits the success of his Olympic athletes with their ability to accept rejection and deal with adversity. Almost invariably, his athletes who did well in the Olympics had experienced some sort of prior setback. They had either been sick or hurt. But it was the ability to overcome these setbacks, the resiliency to snap back, and the single-minded concentration on their goals regardless of what happened, that proved to be the critical factor.

In 1984, Carl Lewis made public his intention to go after Jesse Owens's record of four Olympic gold medals. His announcement became a big media event, and Lewis became an even bigger celebrity. Had Lewis succumbed to the subsequent heavy media demands, however, I suspect he would have been distracted from his goal and not won the four gold medals. Under enormous stress, he maintained his focus and concentration. During the Olympic Games, for instance, the media criticized Lewis for not taking all of his jumps in the long jump. But it was not pointed out, nor did most people realize, that Lewis would be the only competitor on the track on each day of the eight-day track and field competition. In fact, on each day, Lewis was first in every one of his events.

Lewis's performance required tremendous concentration: he had his own considerable goal, he had the eyes of the world on him, and he had the unending demands of the media. But Lewis also had what proved to be the Winning Edge—a single-minded determination to stay focused on his goal. He shut out the rest of the world, and he shut out the media. Obviously he has had to pay for this because he is not a media darling now, but the greater point is that if he had succumbed to media pressures, Carl Lewis might not today be only the second man in history to have won four Olympic gold medals in track the same year.

The Winning Edge manifests itself in different ways. A broad definition of the Winning Edge is simply the definition of success—doing the best job you can, given your potential and your abilities, under the circumstances. When you put success together with talent and luck, you get a winner. Your ability to do the best you can under the circumstances is something over which you have a great deal of control—but beyond that, being able to control winning is impossible.

For example, in the 1984 Olympic Games if you drew lane one around the curve in the 200- or 400-meter dash, circumstances were virtually beyond your control. With the level of talent so even, the handicap of running the tighter turn was decisive enough a factor to prevent you from winning the race. Nobody won out of lane one around the curve. If you were unlucky enough to draw lane one, you could still be a success—that is, you could still do the best job you could—but the odds against your winning were stacked. It was a hard fact of life.

What the Winning Edge always comes down to, therefore, is taking a situation and maximizing your potential within the existing realities—putting yourself in the best possible position of winning. But it can take many different forms not only for different people but also at different times.

Let me give you an example. One of the longest-standing world and Olympic records is in the 400 meters. This record was established in 1968. The person who holds the record is Lee Evans. Evans is a very special case. He won the Olympic gold medal at 400 meters, yet he was only the *fifth* best 400-meter talent on the *U.S.* team. He was the consummate competitor, but Larry James, Vince Mathews (1972 400-meter Olympic champ), Ron Freeman (world record holder of the fastest 400 relay split ever run), and Tommie Smith, among the Americans in 1968, were all more gifted than Evans. Evans, though, got the job done because he would pay whatever price it took to win.

Still, Evans always had a basic fear of Larry James. This fear was so intense that Evans had regular nightmares about James beating him. His phobia about James was entirely justified: James had the nickname "The Burner" for a very good reason.

Between the semifinals and the finals of the 1968 Olympic Games 400 meters in Mexico City, Evans was trying to rest and relax. Try as he might, Evans could not get the specter of Larry James out of his mind. His biggest concern was that perhaps this would finally be the day he would lose to James. Just as Evans had the least self-confidence, James bounded into Evans's room. "Hey, man, have you seen the lane assignments for the finals?" From the gleeful tone of James's voice, Evans knew things were not looking good. With undisguised smugness, James told Evans that Evans had an outer lane while he, James, was inside. As their times were so close, James having the better lane seemed to give him the edge. He knew it, and Evans knew it.

What neither knew at the time, however, was how Evans was ultimately going to react. James, certain he had applied the final "psych," left the room confident. Evans's first reaction was to resign himself to losing. He grew depressed. But suddenly he understood that that was exactly what James wanted to happen. The more Evans thought about it, the angrier he got. Finally, by the time the race came about, Evans was so angry, he would be damned, he thought, before he allowed James's ploy to work.

The result of the race was determined by a few hundredths of a second. Evans was the winner.

James, in trying to psych out Evans, made a logistical error. He gave Evans too much time to react and recover. James may initially have had the Winning Edge but lost it—and in the process provided Evans with precisely what he needed to win the race.

The point here is that no situation is so hopeless that you cannot turn it to your advantage if you simply do not accept its forgone conclusion—what is "commonly expected"—especially if it does not favor you. Lee Evans had a remarkable ability to compete, train hard, and do whatever it took to win. He was able to combine these talents in such a fashion so as to beat just about anyone he met—except for Martin McGrady.

Martin McGrady was one of those athletes a coach has once in a lifetime. I never saw him lose a race he should have won, and I also saw him win many he probably should have lost.

In 1967, the AAU Indoor National Championships were held in Oakland, California. Over lunch I was talking with Lee Evans about his race in the 600 yards. I had seen McGrady run and was impressed with his fluidity and grace. There was no doubt how intense a competitor he was. Evans knew firsthand about McGrady as they had trained together under the legendary Bud Winter at San Jose State University.

I suggested to Evans that the best way to beat a rhythm runner was to make him break his rhythm and stride very late in the race. The best place to do this, Evans and I decided, was on the final turn of the 11-lap indoor track. The turn comes just 80 yards from the finish, at a time when a 600 runner is straining and working for all he's worth. A mishap or mistake here is inevitably disastrous. The strategy was to get the lead and go into the last turn so hard that McGrady, if he attempted to pass, would have to run high on the banked track and risk losing his balance or rhythm or both.

The race began exactly as planned. Evans took the lead with McGrady content to sit on his shoulder. Going into the final turn, with just over 80 yards to go, Evans surged again, as planned, forcing McGrady to move hard and wide into the curve merely to keep up. I could hardly contain myself as I saw the strategy I had devised working perfectly. Things looked even better when McGrady, as anticipated, momentarily lost his rhythm and balance and actually ran up a couple of lanes on the banked track. Evans, being the strong, tough, competitive finisher he was, was virtually assured the victory. No man could catch him. It was obvious to everyone in the arena.

There was, however, one hard head who would not accept this obvious fact. McGrady, from his position high and wide on the banked track, used the incline in the track to generate and launch some momentum. He came down off the turn as if he was shot out of a cannon. His momentum sent him flying down the track, and the roar of the amazed crowd was like a big wave giving a surfer the ride of his life.

McGrady swept past a stunned Lee Evans and flashed a big, wide smile to the crowd as he crossed the finish line. McGrady, known as the "Chairman of the Boards" because of his superiority on indoor board tracks, had just given another shining example of why his nickname was so richly deserved.

The Martin McGrady story does not end here. A couple of years later I saw McGrady at a meet, and we talked about the 1967 AAU Indoor Championship 600. He was amused at the strategy Lee and I had developed to beat him, but was also impressed enough to ask if I would coach him. He had a goal in mind.

The following October, 1969, McGrady called to say he was coming east to train with me. Three days later, at a practice session in Washington, D.C., a 1964 GTO came roaring up. In it sat a smiling McGrady. He had driven nonstop cross-country from California with only his Bible and a map.

McGrady was a real challenge to coach. He and I were very much the "odd couple." Martin was warm, gentle, shy, quiet, and never outwardly upset. He didn't raise his voice in anger or use any phrase stronger than "darn it." On the other hand I was coarse, opinionated, outspoken, and abrupt. It seemed our language preferences were as divergent as our personalities. But strangely enough, we got along well.

Training was going along smoothly until late December that year when McGrady pulled his hamstring. In order to get his mind off his injury, I talked with him about goals and objectives for the coming season.

"Martin, what do you think you can run for the six hundred?" I asked. His reply, like almost everything else about him, surprised me.

"One oh seven five."

I said, "Martin, the world record is one oh nine-flat."

He flashed that smile of his and said, "Yeah, I know what it is."

Of course, he and I both knew what the record was. We also both knew that he was the holder of that record.

"Martin," I said, "that means going out in forty-eight and a half for the four forty and coming back in nineteen seconds for the final lap of one hundred sixty yards!"

"Coach, that's what I can run," he replied. "I'm not sure how it breaks down, but I know I can run that fast."

I thought to myself, "You've done it now. This cowboy thinks he can knock a whole second and a half off the world record, and he expects you to train him to do it. Maybe you can make him feel homesick enough for the sunny weather of San Jose, and he'll leave before both of you make fools of yourselves."

Not having the heart to interject a negative note when McGrady was already depressed about his hamstring injury, in addition to being away from home for the Christmas holidays, I started laying out plans for him to run 1:07.5 for 600 yards indoors. Soon enough, I too began to believe in his quest.

Even now, as I look back on it, I marvel at the arrogance we both had. Here was this injured athlete, missing home, barely having trained for six weeks, and he and his coach are plotting to break the world record by one and a half seconds. We formulated our plans, dreaming out loud.

First, we would destroy the competition so we could concentrate on the 1:07.5. That meant somehow disposing of Lee Evans, the world record holder and Olympic gold medalist (at 400 and 4 × 400).

Second, as we were planning this slaughter of the world record, we would do it before a full house where we would get maximum media coverage. There was only one place to do it: Madison Square Garden in New York—the center of indoor track—at the AAU Indoor Championships. The meet was to be held the last weekend in February. That gave us nine weeks to get McGrady healthy and in shape to dispense with an Olympic legend and to run a new world record.

Undaunted by the folly of it all, we forged ahead. In January there was a meet in Philadelphia at the convention center.

McGrady was anxious to run, but I was uncertain of his fitness, coming off an injury. I opted to hide him on the 4 × 400 relay, wanting to save him embarrassment on the chance he was not yet ready. But the odds seemed stacked against McGrady. Somehow it worked out that he and Larry James, "The Burner," were to run the same leg. This was the same Larry James who was second to Lee Evans in the 1968 Olympic 400 and whose second place time is still the second fastest ever at 400. This was the same talented athlete who caused the great Lee Evans to have nightmares. Furthermore, this was Philadelphia, hometown of James, who was attending Villanova University.

The 4 × 400 was the final event on the program because it is the most electrifying and exciting. By the time McGrady got the relay baton, James was already 10 yards ahead of him, and the race appeared to be no contest. Besides, the small track at the convention center, three laps per 440, made passing a quality runner almost impossible because of the short straights and sharp, banked curves.

As the race progressed, McGrady moved up a bit on James in the first lap, but it was little cause for concern. James, it seemed, was just allowing a little drama to develop. On the second lap, as McGrady passed where the team stood, cheering and screaming, he smiled and raised the baton, as if signaling he was about to make his move. The gesture was not lost on James's hometown crowd, who responded with an even louder, more intense show of support for the Burner.

James, sensing the moment, decided it was time to assert himself and put the race completely out of reach. He was in good position because one of those sharp, steep curves was just ahead, and a few scant yards out of the curve was the finish line. But before he could execute, McGrady was on top of him, moving with incredible fluidity and grace. Going into the turn, McGrady glided up on James's shoulder.

Knowledgeable people know that to attempt to pass an athlete like James in this type of situation is tactical suicide.

Yet, in a flash, McGrady swept up and past James on the curve, then continued on, powering past the finish line. The crowd went silent, and for one precious, delicious instant, a strange and quiet shock hung in the air. Then the crowd erupted with cheers and applause for the maverick McGrady as he jogged effortlessly around the track for his victory lap.

Bolstered by our success against Larry James, Martin McGrady and I began our serious training for establishing a new world record. We had six weeks to do it. There was still another major obstacle in the way of a clear shot at the record—Lee Evans. It was our feeling that we had to neutralize Evans as a factor when we made our big push for the 1:07.5 time at the Indoor National Championships at Madison Square Garden. We wanted to eliminate him as a serious threat, leaving us free and clear to focus on the record.

Keep in mind, the person we were so lightly dismissing was one of the all-time great competitors, the world record holder at 400 and 4 × 400 and holder of the world best at the 500. (World records at that time were not recognized from indoor competitions, so I refer to Evans's mark in the 500 as the world best.) But we were on a roll, and nothing seemed too big a challenge or barrier.

The strategy was to run all sorts of different tactics against Evans in the smaller competitions leading up to the big race. We would defeat him by running in front the entire way and holding him off at the end. When he caught on, we would defeat him by running from behind and kicking past him at the end.

The plan worked with amazing success, but it was McGrady who pulled it off. This was not an easy task since Evans was one of the sport's fiercest competitors and came on at the end with a blistering rush. But McGrady would not be beaten and outkicked Evans every time.

These were heady days. The result of all these races was *four* new world records for McGrady in a *three*-week span! One weekend, McGrady broke the record *twice*. But, most important, Lee Evans was essentially neutralized because he was absolutely confused as to what tactic to use against McGrady.

I had trained McGrady so that he would be able to run the first 440 in 48.5 and hopefully be able to come back in 19-flat for the last 160 yards—which was where the race's time would be determined. In practice we ran all sorts of workouts designed to fatigue McGrady in different ways. But no matter how fatigued he was or what kind of fatigue he was feeling—whether rubber-legged or booty-locked—he would finish off each session with a 160 in 19.0 or better. We did it so often that his body grew calloused and he grew confident in his ability to do the job.

Finally the big night arrived. For several weeks the McGrady-Evans duels had been the talk of the indoor circuit, and the national championships had gained more attention and significance as a result. Everyone looked forward to the battle between the lithe, fluid Martin McGrady and the hard-charging, relentless Lee Evans. For McGrady, of course, the new world record was just out of reach, and for Evans, nothing would be sweeter than to beat McGrady at Madison Square Garden before a packed house.

McGrady was confident. He had behind him the success he had enjoyed over Evans in all of their other races. He had his terrific time intervals in practice—proof aplenty that he could run the critical last lap in a target time of 19.0.

At the gun, McGrady went immediately to the front. He was not challenged; Evans was content to let McGrady spend himself and beat him with a surge at the end. As McGrady passed the 440 mark I yelled his split. It was exactly 48.5. McGrady looked at me and winked. A wry smile creased his face, and he proceeded to run the last lap with new verve.

Evans never really came close. McGrady was so focused on his goal—his running style smooth, effortless, graceful, more like a ballet dancer than a jock—that the race was, in a sense, no contest. When McGrady crossed the finish line first, the excitement came not from the race but from the feat he had accomplished. The crowd of 19,000 roared. McGrady's time was 1:07.6; we had missed his prediction by one-tenth of a second, but his time was certainly a new world record. Evans came in second—with a time under McGrady's old world record.

I have often wondered if McGrady would have gotten his predicted time if he had not smiled. I have wondered what the time would have been if we had selected a bigger and faster track. But I am consoled by the fact that the record is the longest-standing indoor record on the books despite the fact that the race has been run thousands of times by talented athletes on better tracks than the 160 at Madison Square Garden.

The Winning Edge here was careful planning, proper training, and great execution.

2
THE PSYCHOLOGY OF RUNNING

In the exploits of runners who demonstrate the Winning Edge, it is obvious that these people do not prevail by simple physical activity alone. In almost every case there is a psychological factor lurking in the background. Talent, tenacity, and hard work are always important, but psychology is ultimately the determining and limiting factor.

In 1952, as a high school senior, I ran the 100-yard dash in 10.9 seconds—which was slow even then; the world record for men at that time was 9.3. Today, at 100 *meters,* Evelyn Ashford holds the world record for women at 10.75 seconds. That's a faster time than mine, although her distance is almost *ten yards* longer. By 1958, I had made myself into a fair, journeyman-type sprinter. I had learned to exploit advantages that circumstances presented in a race, gaining the psychological Winning Edge. I was placing in most of the major indoor meets and even won on rare occasions. As background reference: The point here is that speed *can* be developed and enhanced, contrary to the school of so-called natural athletes. Later, at graduate school at the University of Chicago, I was a teammate and friend of Ira Murchison.

At that time, Murchison was without a doubt the fastest sprinter indoors. The idea of my beating him was scoffed at by the experts and knowledgeable track "gurus"—something which only fueled my desire to do exactly that. Ira's being a very close friend added even more incentive. I looked at the situation. Here was a man at the height of his career. No ordinary effort was going to beat him. I had to come up with something special if I was going to pull it off. My determination and deviousness knew no boundary.

I will never forget the fateful race. It was at the Holiday Invitational Meet of the Chicago Track Club. Murchison and I had both qualified first in our heats, he was typically a tenth of a second faster than I. For the final we were lined up in adjoining lanes. On either side of us were two white sprinters. The starter was white as well.

Now, in 1958, before the comic routines of Dick Gregory (who was also a teammate in the Chicago Track Club) and Richard Pryor, there were certain words that blacks did not use to each other in mixed company. To each other, such terms might be brotherly, friendly, even affectionate, but they could easily be misconstrued in the presence of others. It was a notion I seized upon. As Murchison and I started to our marks, I turned to him and whispered our usual banter: "Little nigger, I'm going to whip your ass." And as usual, he gave me one of his patented cocky, oh-yeah? smiles.

As we took our marks, the crowd grew quiet. The starter gave the command, "get set." At that moment, in that silence, I began to hiss—"Nigger! Nigger! Nigger!"—loud enough for those around us to hear. Everyone froze except for the starter and me. He fired the gun, I bolted from the blocks, and Murchison never caught me. I made him vulnerable, the tactic broke his concentration, and he let me momentarily paralyze him.

The point is twofold. I turned the negative of racism to my positive advantage, but, more important, he *allowed* himself to get psychologically trapped. The stimulus was mine, but the response was entirely his. The damage was done by himself.

From that day on, Murchison lost the psychological Winning Edge over me at 60 yards. He could beat me soundly at 50 yards, 100 yards, 100 meters, but he never beat me again at 60. He was permanently caught in the trap.

In retelling this story in later years, many have questioned the "fairness" of this tactic. Every competitive event has a "psych" factor involved. But the "psych" factor can only work against those that allow it. There are always distractions and things to get in the way of doing well, the task of the great competitive athlete is to overcome, defeat, even turn these into "plus" factors rather than "psych" factors. Whether what I did was sporting or fair is not the point. The point is that the Winning Edge requires a certain mindset and strength in order to assure success.

All of the great runners I know, in fact all of the great competitive athletes I have known over the years, have one thing in common: they have the need and the ability to compensate for real or perceived deficiencies. In order for a great athlete to push himself or herself to the ultimate, there has to be an abnormal need present somewhere. Simply put, well-adjusted, happy people do not make great athletic competitors. Great athletes become so insecure at times of great stress and competition that there is tremendous need to compensate, to prove themselves.

The difference between great athletes and not-so-great athletes, therefore, is not the ability, training, coaching, or even physical tools. The difference is the ability and need to perform well under extreme pressure when insecurity is at its highest. The greater the competitor, the greater the ability to do what is required—and more—under duress. The greater the competitor, the greater the *need* to do what is required under great stress.

The secret to competitive success is the ability to convert the pressure and insecurity into the powerful force it can become. Great runners have the ability to harness the electricity of the moment, the forces of extreme levels of stress, and then to convert them to their own positive value. A great race is not solely an athletic event; it is theater and drama at its highest gut level—with the performers shamelessly demonstrating their psychological needs. Successful runners revel in performing before the crowds because they need the acceptance and love of people as much as actors do. Both have rehearsed their parts countless times, and both are well schooled as to what and how to perform. The great ones go one step beyond what the script calls for: they reach deep inside themselves, to get the extra flow of energy that will single them out as superior to their fellow performers.

It is easy to see the Winning Edge in Muhammad Ali, perhaps the greatest athlete/actor of all. Before major fights in the early part of his career, his pulse rate was so high that doctors feared for his well-being. Before his first professional championship fight with Sonny Liston, his resting pulse was reported to be over 200. But Ali was the consummate athlete, and he performed his craft the way he had been trained. The result was a knockout with a punch that many people watching the fight missed. Even after seeing it on replay, people were stunned that Ali could have done that much damage with just one short punch.

Ali had done with his adrenaline what we have witnessed others do in a similar state. He converted the energy from the excitement and electricity of the event into an awesome personal power. This is the same reservoir of strength that accounts for the grandmother who lifted the car off of her pinned grandchild without taking the time to think about the impossibility of the task. The adrenaline of the moment was so overwhelming, her basic concerns so strong, that she was able to accomplish what under almost every other circumstance would be impossible.

As I have pointed out, training, coaching, and ability are only some of the ingredients necessary for success. One of the most critical aspects of winning is knowing how to go about winning. Many people who want to do well and are ready to do well, fail because they have the inappropriate competitive approach.

Competitions can be approached in more than one way, and athletes should seek out the approach that is right for them. For example, some people can be motivated by the idea of competing *mano-a-mano*. In this case, the athlete has the feeling, "If they can do it, then I know I can do it, probably even better." Or feels, "I really want this and I'm going to get it and I'm not going to let anyone stand in my way." This type of personality is goal-oriented and is naturally competitive and aggressive. For such people the goal is the all-consuming aspect. The methodology is secondary.

Other people may do well when presented with a particular task that they are confident they can perform. If they are trained to run five minutes a mile for a given distance, for example, and they focus on doing that, rather than worrying what the opposition is doing, they tend to do better. They appear less concerned about competing and more caught up in the task. When matched against stronger personalities, they tend to subordinate their own talents and abilities, and glorify that of others. This type of personality is task-oriented. Such athletes do not usually do well when confronted with competition on a person-to-person basis. For these people, executing a simple, almost impersonal task is easy. Methodology is the primary concern.

Although a runner is predominantly one way or the other, there are times when he or she will switch attitudes. That can be foolhardy. The best and most consistent results come from runners who know their personality and who perfect their approach. In major competition, switching over can be a problem. I have seen people change their approach with disastrous results.

Approach changeover can be seen in the example of Mary Slaney and Ruth Wysocki after the 1984 U.S. Olympic trials. One can never know exactly what goes on in another coach's or athlete's mind, but let me hazard a guess because what I witnessed had such classic approach changeover symptoms.

In 1983, Mary Slaney swept both the 1500 and 3000 meter races at the World Championships. But more important, she swept the two events by defeating the best in the world, the East Germans and the Russians included. This impressive feat established her as the number one female middle-distance runner in the world. But at the U.S. Olympic trials in June of 1984, Slaney lost the 1500 meter race to Ruth Wysocki. This set up a psychological situation in which, to my mind, both were affected negatively at the 1984 Olympic Games.

Mary Slaney had almost always won head-to-head battles with her opponents. The famous picture of her out-competing and out-leaning the Russian runner at the finish of the 3000-meter race in the world championships in Helsinki with the Russian woman falling in her effort to beat Slaney, is a perfect example of Slaney's will to win and her confidence in her ability to do so. This was all changed, however, when Slaney lost to Wysocki at the U.S. Olympic trials. In this case, Slaney had been beaten by an American—something which had not happened since 1973—and her confidence was badly undermined.

What is ironic about this loss is that at the trials, not only did Slaney have to run more races to qualify for the finals than at the world championships, but her times at the trials were faster than they were the year before in winning the World Championships. In addition, her coach, Dick Brown, had trained her to run the 1500-meter final at the U.S. trials in 4:00.0. She was less than one second off the target time—which can be traced to the fact that the race went out in 65–66 seconds for the opening 400 meters rather than the 63–64 pace Dick Brown had wanted for her, and a time she routinely ran in her prior races.

So there was really no need for Slaney to be any more concerned after the U.S. trials than she was after the world championships. Her times were better than they'd been the year before, she was just slightly off schedule from what her coach had planned, and she had had a much tougher time at the trials because of the way the events were scheduled. It also turned out that her second place time in the 1500 at the trials would have won the final at the Olympic Games. So Mary had every reason to be confident and certain about herself.

A task-oriented person would have taken the defeat in stride and been grateful that it came before the Olympic Games. Further, he or she would have seen the loss in terms of task, not running the first lap as fast as usual. But not so for goal-oriented Slaney. Even considering that Slaney's times and the conditions under which they were achieved were a solid basis for confidence, almost arrogance, the fact that stuck out in her mind, according to my reckoning, was that her goal of winning the U.S. Olympic trials had not been realized.

She was crushed that she had been beaten—and by an American—despite the fact that she had every other reason to feel satisfaction and confidence. After all, the monkey was off her back now that it had happened. Furthermore, it was obvious that her coach's program was working almost to perfection, and, given time, he would have come up with the answers to what she needed to run even faster. As fate would have it, she would not have had to run faster to win the Olympics anyway. But that was in the future. What haunted her was the fact that she had been beaten by another individual.

Ruth Wysocki had come into the U.S. Olympic trials completely relaxed. Just a few races before the trials she was still trying to qualify. Being in great shape and with talent, she had the perfect attitude—for her—to do well at the U.S. trials. After she had made the Olympic team in the 800, I asked her what her plans were for the 1500. "Oh, I don't really know," she said. "All I wanted to do was to make it here in the first place and see what I could do. I guess I'll take the 1500 as it comes and see what happens." She was not concerned about the other people in the race, but was simply running and doing her best.

This was a classic task-oriented approach, but after she defeated Mary Slaney, things changed. All of a sudden she was the person who had beaten the world's leading distance runner in women's track and field. She became a personality, and people began to expect and demand results from her.

Wysocki was not in an athlete versus athlete mode, and she changed her orientation from a task-type competitor into a goal-type competitor. She was now being measured not against herself and her ability to perform tasks alone but was thrust into a situation where her running became a rivalry. She began to worry about her competition.

The interim between the U.S. Olympic trials in the latter part of June and the Olympic Games in early August proved to be the unmaking of both Wysocki and Slaney. The time off let them get mired in their uncomfortable new approach modes, rather than reassess their own performances and get back to the psychological approaches that had worked for them all along.

This resulting awkwardness was clearly evident at the games. Both runners were quite different from what they had been five weeks earlier. Neither had the light touch, the spring, that they had at the trials. Both were running "in" the track rather than "on" it.

Slaney did win the U.S. trials in the 3000 meters. Then, she opted to drop out of the 1500 meters, in which Wysocki had earlier beaten her, and concentrate on the 3000. This was probably the first manifestation of an approach change. The first overt sign of needless panic and overconcern.

It is interesting to note that before Slaney was tripped in the 3000 by Zola Budd, she had already been bumped by Budd earlier on the turn. In the past, when Slaney was challenged at any point in the race, she would have instinctively attempted to move away from the challenger. She would not have worried about "saving it" or worried about her reserve. She would have run with élan, relying on the deep confidence in her ability to defeat anyone who had the audacity to challenge her one-on-one. In this case, instead of accepting the challenge, she chose to remain where she was. Then Budd pressed the attack a bit more and moved over into Slaney's space.

There is no doubt in my mind that Slaney was technically fouled, that Budd should have been called on the violation. As a matter of fact, even before the race was concluded, after her fall I sprinted to the protest trailer and watched a rerun of the race. Convinced she was fouled, I filed a protest that was initially upheld. Then a very strange thing happened. After I left, satisfied that the U.S. protest was going to be upheld, the protest ruling was mysteriously reversed. We were never told how or why, despite heated and intense requests for answers. On the other hand, Slaney should have been more assertive tactically. She should have pushed Budd away or simply picked up the pace. I have seen her do both many times—with authority and success. But her confidence was not the same as it had been in the past. Now she was focusing on accomplishing a task, rather than not allowing herself to be beaten by anyone. Slaney, in her more natural goal-oriented, athlete-to-athlete mode, would have done what it took to keep Budd off her. But, alas, the U.S. Olympic trials on the same track just a few weeks earlier had changed all that.

The same was true with Wysocki in the 1500 meters. With Slaney out of the race, the new goal-oriented pressure proved too debilitating for Wysocki. The burden on her mind was too heavy, her time was nowhere near her best, and she finished way out of the running.

Successful runners have established solid identities for good reason, and their training, tactics, and talent should all be consistent with that winning identity. To alter this identity is to negate their best effort. When Slaney and Wysocki's images of themselves became inconsistent with their actual identities, they failed.

The point is that you must have a clear picture of yourself in order to exploit your abilities and to maximize your potential. If your image is in focus, then your mind and body will act in concert with that image. When this mental image is blurred and confused, your physical performance will reflect that confusion. If the confusion gets too great, an athlete can "freeze" or become, for a moment, physically catatonic. Many competitive athletes have frozen in critical situations, not because of physical weakness or character flaw but because they do not have a clear picture of their approach and their abilities.

In a similar fashion, "lazy" or undermotivated people lack a clear image of themselves and their tasks. Consequently, their performance is indifferent, ambivalent, and uncertain. There is no such thing as a "naturally" lazy person. Simply observe young kids at play. What is "natural" is activity, curiosity, and challenge. "Laziness" is either learned and developed, or the misinterpretation of the observer. In order to improve, a runner must face several issues. The runner first has to know exactly what it is he or she wants. Next, in terms of what is wanted, the runner must make an assessment of his or her abilities. The runner must determine if getting what he or she wants requires substantial changes. Finally, the runner must decide whether he or she really wants to make the changes. In too many cases a runner does not improve, simply because he or she is unwilling to face the facts involved in improving.

Recreational runners who try to switch over to competitive running are a special case in point. Often the attempt ends in failure and disappointment. Why? Because they refuse to accept the fact that their goals have changed. They do not want to take on a different attitude about their running, yet they expect different results. They do not realize that different goals require different training—that, in particular, long, slow, distance-type training alone will not produce winning results in races where speed and technique are important, however long the race.

People cannot expect to improve only on their own terms. Without a basic change in mental outlook and physical training, improvement cannot occur, and there is little likelihood of success. A new challenge must be met on the terms appropriate to that challenge. Success at one level—as a recreational runner, for example—is no guarantee of success on another—as a competitive runner—unless the new demands are known, accepted, and mastered.

The similarities between an Olympic champion and a weekend warrior far outweigh the differences. People have far more in common with a world record holder than they imagine. There are many with the ability and potential to meet the demands of being a champion, but very few are willing to seek the knowledge and find the confidence to accept the challenge. The Winning Edge is not waiting for success but working hard and intelligently for it.

3

THE PHYSICS AND PHYSIOLOGY OF RUNNING

If you neglect the basic mechanics of running, it will lead inevitably to injury and frustration. Many of the early advocates of running placed great emphasis on its ethereal aspects, making little of the crucial physical and physiological aspects. Running was viewed as some kind of "spiritual" experience. As a result, many of the early converts to running and jogging later turned to other activities because they were not only disappointed, they often sustained needless injuries. The paradox is that only through the development and maintenance of proper mechanics can those inner values and "elevated" experiences of running be regularly and routinely achieved.

If you want satisfaction and safety in your running, if you want to improve your time and distance, then you must observe the basic laws of physics. This may require a reexamination of what you are already doing, and it may also require a new look at some of the myths and stereotypes surrounding running.

All of us have the capacity to run faster. All of us have the capacity to run longer. This holds true for everyone from the world's fastest human down to the five-hour marathoner. And it is likewise true that everyone has the capacity to run longer and faster, to run faster and longer, and to run longer faster.

If one is a sprinter, the object is to run faster longer. If one is a distance runner, the object is to run longer faster. These two classes of runners are directly related, because the problems that both groups face are solved by learning the physics of running. Most distance runners, however, have neglected speed as a primary concern, when, in fact, the secrets that are the sprinter's stock and trade can unlock the secret of distance running. You will find that the same principles apply.

The chief limitation on a sprinter's speed is the fear of falling. If you have the desire to sprint but are not willing to risk falling, you are not going to run very fast for very long.

At the beginning of a race, a sprinter is suspended over the track in an elongated leaning position. When he bursts from the starting block, he applies a tremendous amount of horizontal force, which builds up his speed and momentum. A sprinter will go fastest when he achieves maximum horizontal velocity, but just as this speed is approached, the sprinter does an odd thing. He begins to straighten his body and become more erect. Thus he applies less horizontal force and more vertical force, which has the effect of slowing him down. Since the sprinter wants to achieve maximum horizontal velocity, it stands to reason that the sprinter would want to maintain the leaning position as long as possible—and work against what seems a natural inclination to become more vertical as he sprints down the track.

Biomechanics explains this phenomenon in terms of the length of time the foot is in contact with the ground. As the sprinter gathers speed, his feet spend less time on the ground. But when the sprinter's feet spend less time on the ground, his posture becomes more erect. Consequently, as sprinters run faster they are less effective in applying horizontal force. The biomechanical explanation describes *what* happens but does not explain *why* it happens.

Man's instinct is to maintain equilibrium and balance. When a sprinter starts to rotate forward and down at speeds up to 30 miles per hour, the psyche's natural fear of falling and the desire for equilibrium takes over, causing the sprinter to change a perilous situation into a more acceptable one.

The sprinter who can defy or delay the "fear of falling" mechanism the longest is going to run faster longer. Studies have shown that the top end speed of an elite sprinter and a mediocre sprinter is not significantly different. They can both achieve about the same maximum velocity. Yet the elite sprinter can get to that speed and hold it a tad longer than the rest. It is the elite sprinter's ability to block out the command from the psyche that says, "Fool, slow down, this is too dangerous!"

That accounts for the difference. The fear of falling is the ultimate limitation on speed. Some people seem to have the ability to defy this fear more than others, but it is a talent that anyone can learn.

First, you have to convince yourself that falling is not necessarily as painful or dangerous as it seems. This can be achieved by simple rolling and tumbling exercises and drills, which are incorporated into pre-workout or stretching sessions. This contact with the ground will ease the mind and, in turn, enhance speed—even for the long distance runner.

The second and more direct way of overcoming the fear of falling while running at high speeds is to sprint down a slight incline while in a leaning position. This drill allows the runner to reach new speeds, with little effort. At the same time that it exaggerates actual physical conditions that are cause of the fear. Success here retards the mechanism that leads the sprinter to right himself. Unlike towing or pulling drills, which supposedly do the same thing, running down an incline in a leaning position trains the mind and the body to be comfortable at running at high speeds. When an athlete is towed or pulled, the athlete actually leans back against the pull and assumes a more upright position. In a race, this is exactly the position you should avoid.

* * *

Despite all of the science involved, in the final analysis, what makes running special is that each person does it with his or her own style. True, your style has to be consistent with certain basic principles, but you can only run well if you run in a way that uniquely capitalizes on your strengths and minimizes or compensates for your deficiencies. So that you can recognize your strengths and weaknesses, it is critical that you know the roles that various parts of the body play in running. (For exercises that address specific needs, see also Chapter 6: Omnibus Drills and Exercises.)

When you run or walk, you apply force against the ground, the ground resists that force and applies a reciprocal force in the opposite direction—upon your body. Since all reciprocating forces applied to and received from the ground pass through the foot, the foot naturally becomes of paramount importance in running. It is a fact that is so obvious that it is often overlooked.

Despite its importance, the foot has been misunderstood and abused not only by runners but by shoe manufacturers who, regardless of their hype, must take the blame for unhealthy shoe designs. The simple, basic function of shoes should be to provide friction with the running or walking surface and to provide strategic support. Most shoes do not do this. Instead, they disguise the size of feet, convey more style than comfort, and most critically, actually deform and weaken feet. It seems that we have not been wearing shoes as much as shoes have been wearing us.

For the runner, shoes have become a cast, even a coffin, for the foot. When a working body part is encased and its natural movement restricted, conditions are created for what is called "disuse atrophy." What this means is that if a body part does not work the way it is supposed to, it becomes weak through misuse or lack of use. Think of what happens to an arm or a leg encased in a cast. The tissue in that limb grows smaller and weaker, while the bone density lessens and the bone becomes brittle. Most shoes, although they are not as rigid as a cast, effectively cause the same damage to the foot if worn over a long period of time. This is especially true of shoes that are too tight and restrictive.

Shoe companies, in a mad dash for profits during the running boom, produced a full range of models that purported to answer all kinds of problems. More often than not shoes were designed to look like Formula One racing cars, with their heels elevated and flared rear ends, with slick state-of-the-art polyurethane platforms. As a result, shoe companies created the very problems they ballyhooed as curing. Moreover, like a drug that is taken to ease one symptom and then creates its own dependency, inferior athletic footwear causes similar addiction.

The foot must be a very strong lever if it is to carry out its role in running. Regardless of how well trained or ambitious an athlete is, he is ultimately limited by the weakness of his feet. When you run, you multiply the body's weight several times, so the foot has to be fortified enough to handle the extra pressure. For example, if you gain five pounds, then the foot must be capable of transmitting that additional force to the ground, absorbing the force back from the ground, and redirecting that force upward and forward. Depending on how fast you are running, those five new pounds of force may add up to twenty to twenty-five pounds of additional stress that the foot has to sustain.

Unfortunately the shoe industry does not acknowledge this basic principle. When the running boom first hit middle-aged Americans who were not particularly active or healthy, companies designed supposedly revolutionary shoes that would allow them to run more than was wise, given their level of fitness. Soles were padded to absorb shock and heels elevated to "protect" the Achilles tendon, instead of letting the foot itself, as it does in more basic shoe styles, determine its natural limits. Injury and breakdown were inevitable.

The stress of prolonged running became absorbed inside the padded shoe rather than being transmitted to the running surface. A person *was* able to run longer (though not with reasonable expectation of good foot health), but he or she could run no faster because the shoes dissipated the additional reciprocal forces needed for greater speed.

Soles were so thick and cumbersome that they bent only in areas where the shoes were weakest; nor did these areas always coincide with the points at which the foot wanted to bend. This combination of unhealthy forces applied to the foot resulted, not uncommonly, in stress fractures. The padded soles, moreover, did not let the foot work fully and properly. Through disuse atrophy, it grew weaker rather than stronger. And as the shoes allowed runners to run longer distances, the already weakened foot was overtaxed and abused further.

As a result of running too-long distances, inflammation of the Achilles tendon often set in. To deal with this, shoe companies elevated the heel, which effectively shortened the Achilles tendon, cutting down on both its stress and inflammation. Since people had already been wearing shoes with elevated heels, this, coupled with their relative inactivity, caused the Achilles tendon, through disuse atrophy, to weaken even more. It is interesting to note that before the running boom, when running shoes were for active, athletic people, shoes had no built-up heel, and Achilles tendonitis was rare.

Instability was another side effect of the elevated heel. Any time the center of gravity is raised, instability is the result. For already-overstressed new runners, this became another problem to contend with.

Addressing the *symptoms* of these problems, while not dealing with the problems, shoe companies radically changed the basic design of their shoes.

To attack the instability problem, shoe companies developed flared heels. Flared heels were simply a longer lever through which forces could be applied. The longer the lever, the more potential for greater force being applied. The application of greater force, however, caused lateral movement that resulted in ankle, knee, and hip problems, not to mention muscle and bone problems in the foot.

The catch was that runners who wore these feet destroyers became dependent on them. Their sophisticated shoes produced ailments and problems that only other altered shoes could correct. Heel lifts, padded midsoles, and other accessories were available for treating feet that were damaged beyond recall.

Since shoes are responsible for much of the weakness in the feet, walking and light running without them is the most sensible and natural way of correcting and strengthening them. Such a barefoot program is important for the foot itself as well as the rest of the body. When the foot cannot perform its proper function, the body seeks to redistribute that load

Running without shoes in grass or sand is a very good way to naturally strengthen the feet. This enables them to get the proper "feel" and feedback necessary to strengthen and develop proper support.

somewhere else, usually to the connective tissues up and down the leg, but also to the shins, knee, hip, and lower back. Many running injuries can be traced to weak feet.

Here are some pointers to keep in mind:

• When you walk barefoot, make an effort to roll high up on the balls of the foot, starting from a flat-footed position. Roll up on the outside of the foot for part of the time and on the inside of the foot for the remainder.

• Walk flat-footed. This will stretch your Achilles tendon and allow the foot to strengthen itself through its natural full range of motion. As elevated heels have prevented this strengthening, this exercise is crucial. The foot in this case actually works as a lever. In the function of running, the elevated heel offers only inefficient lever action. A flat foot, or better yet, a negative heel, gives the most mechanical efficiency, the best lever. (This is why there is a legal limit as to the amount of negative heel high jumpers and long jumpers can create.)

• Other important exercises for strengthening the foot include toe curls, picking up marbles with your toes, rolling up a towel using your toes, massaging your feet by rolling them over a bottle, as well as resistance-type exercises which include toe raisers with weights.

In order for the foot to work efficiently, it must be placed down properly upon landing. In running there are four basic positions for the foot.

The first position is touch-down, which is when the foot first comes in contact with the running surface. The point of contact should be slightly on the outside edge of the foot, just behind the little toe. It is a mistaken notion of many runners that to run long distance, they need to run heel-to-toe, as if they were walking. For sprinters as well as marathon runners, it's simply bad, unnatural mechanics.

It is easy to approximate the optimal point of landing. While standing, raise one foot forward, about nine inches, as

The foot is shown just before touchdown. Notice how it is angled to allow the runner to land on the outside edge, just behind the mid-foot position.

if running in place. Relax the ankle joint and allow your foot to assume its natural position. Your foot will droop slightly down and forward. You will notice that your foot will land midfoot and not heel first. Your foot will also be tilted down on the outside—an indication of touch-down first on the outside edge of the foot, the natural spot being behind the little toe.

The same position as in the photograph on the previous page. Shown here from another angle, to stress the importance of proper foot strike. Many injuries result from improper foot placement.

The second position is the support position, which is when the heel has come to rest on the ground and the foot is supporting the full weight of the body. This is a dangerous position for people with weak feet because when the time from touch-down to support is accelerated, the foot is unable to sustain the force. The body overrotates toward the center of the foot, and ultimately all the weight ends up resting on the inside of the foot. (Picture, for example, an ice skater with weak ankles.)

This is the full support phase with the foot flat on the ground and the rest of the body advancing forward over the foot. Notice the flexion and relaxation that allow for more shock to dissipate throughout the body and joints.

This condition is called pronation, and the popular treatment is to use orthotic supports in the shoe to prevent overrotation. Orthotics range in price from a few dollars to a few hundred dollars, although the amount you pay is not always proportional to the quality of the product. Moreover, the artificial support only acts as a sop to the symptom. It does very little toward curing the condition, and, in fact, tends rather to create its own need cycle.

So-called hard orthotics simply redirect the shock of impact and cause breakdown somewhere else. Probably the best orthotic is a soft one, made of silicon gel, that most closely approximates the density and viscosity of the foot. The best cure for pronation, though, is to strengthen the feet rather than to prolong their weaknesses with soft shoes or soft or hard orthotics.

During the support position, the upper body should be rotating forward with a tilt toward the center so that you can get the most advantage of the push-off—the third of the three basic positions for the foot. At push-off, the body should rotate forward far enough for the foot to maintain contact with the ground as well as apply and receive maximum force.

The fuller the range of movement, the more mechanically sound running is going to be. Many distance runners and sprinters "hot-foot" it. They pull their foot off the running surface before the foot has rolled through the fullest possible range of movement. One reason for this premature push-off is that an elevated heel gives the Achilles tendon bad kinetic information, and the tendon kicks in too soon. Another reason is that the foot is weak. The third reason is psychological. Many sprinters and distance runners feel that foot turnover is the key to running fast. In reality, this is only half true; there is also the matter of distance.

When push-off is completed, the toes should be pointed back in the direction the foot has just come. Ideally, rotation should come directly up over the big toe because then the

Here the body has rotated forward and over the foot. Notice the very clean angles of the knee bend, arm bend, and overall posture.

At push off, the body is rotated forward and the foot continues to apply force through the full range of motion of the foot.

High heel recovery is essential for the best biomechanical technique, even in middle and long distance running.

foot is acting as the longest possible lever and will function for the maximum effective time in which to apply force and get it back.

Enter the critical role of the Achilles tendon, a tissue that helps the foot, ankle, and leg absorb force. It does its most important work after the foot has gone through the touch-down, support, and push-off positions and before it enters the fourth position or recovery phase—which occurs when the heel of the foot is pulled up from the ground and tucked under the buttocks.

At this juncture, the Achilles tendon, if it is doing its job properly, is stretched its full length. This movement allows it to receive the necessary kinetic feedback and set up what is called a stretch reflex. This reflex helps to lift the heel forward and upward to the buttocks and accelerate the leg swing. When tissue is stretched, it tends to snap back with more force and power than its natural tensile strength would tend to indicate. The farther the Achilles tendon is stretched, the more vigorous the reflexive pull back and resolution leg swing.

Imagine how this process is reduced when you have a shortened and weakened Achilles tendon because of wearing shoes with elevated heels. Assume that the effective length of the Achilles tendon is four inches. If you have a heel that is elevated by ½ inch that means that you have lost 12½ percent of the length of the Achilles tendon. This loss is substantial, especially if it occurs over a long period of time and especially if only heels of increasingly elevated proportions will compensate.

The Achilles tendon must be kept healthy, elongated, elastic, and strong, because the stretch reflex it sets up can give you a free ride, so to speak. One of the ways to get the Winning Edge, is to find where your free rides are and exploit them. Any time you find a reflex movement, or a movement which acts like one, you should take advantage of it. Reflex actions are involuntary, so they do not require any thought and do not register on the body's meter. There is no conscious awareness of fatigue. In addition, they are usually stronger and more powerful than voluntary actions using muscles of comparable size and type.

One of the principal goals of training is to determine how to use the neural pathways so that the movements they trigger become reflexive. The fact that the Achilles tendon starts the heel upward as an involuntary movement is important. If the reflex is strong enough, it will allow the heel to recover very high and close to the buttocks. This is the most efficient way for the leg to swing through—high and tight to the buttocks.

For years, many runners have had the erroneous notion that a low heel recovery is more efficient than high heel recovery, supposedly because it requires less energy. In particular, it was the case with people with weak Achilles tendons and weak feet who found it necessary to shuffle along, barely lifting their heels off the ground. They could not do anything else because they were handicapped. The fact is, however, that bringing the heel up to the buttocks requires *less* overall energy than shuffling. When the Achilles tendon does not do its job, other muscles must kick in and do the work. When the Achilles tendon does its job properly, these other muscles are freed to do their own work.

Another advantage of a high heel recovery is an additional free ride. There is a basic concept of physics which states that if a radius is moving around an axis, shortening that radius will accelerate the movement of the radius by the square of how much you have shortened it. With a low heel recovery, your entire leg acts as the radius with the axis at your hip. With a high heel recovery, only your upper leg acts as the radius because the lower leg is bent and recovered behind the upper leg. The bent leg in a high heel recovery therefore has a greater forward acceleration than a relatively straight leg.

A good way to visualize this is to watch figure skaters just before they go into a fast spin. They begin with their free leg and arms extended. As they bring their free leg and arms in closer to the axis—the center of their bodies—they spin at a dizzying speed. When the skaters want to stop or slow the spin down, they merely extend their arms and leg again to increase their radius. Simply put, it is easier to move a short radius or limb than it is to move a long radius or limb. Contrast the low heel recovery (long radius) with the high heel recovery (short radius) and see which is easier to move. A high heel recovery is clearly the more efficient of the two.

The force of the leg swinging up is partially transmitted to the foot pressing against the ground, causing it to exert more force, to distort more, and to snap back with a reflex action that increases the thrust off the ground. The extra momentum generated by the stretch reflex is used to swing the leg up, and the cycle can begin again. This is another case of a free ride.

The brisk leg movement caused by the shortened leg length also helps in balance, an important factor in running. Anyone who has tried to master a bicycle realizes that when it is moving slowly it is more difficult to balance than when it is moving faster. The same applies to various body parts that move. If the legs and arms are moving fast, then it is easier to balance the body.

If the foot and Achilles tendon are to operate efficiently, there must be a strong yet flexible ankle joint. Movement, or a lack of movement, in this joint determines the range of motion you can get out of the foot. Like the elevated heel, a weak or stiff ankle joint will in turn weaken the foot and Achilles tendon and limit their ability to function properly. It is the ankle joint that must help sustain impact, dissipate shock, and protect the shin bone from collapse. If the ankle joint is unhealthy, then the shock creates havoc in the joint itself, damaging the tissue, before passing the trauma on up to the knee, hips, and lower back. Repeated impact to a weak ankle joint will eventually result in painful calcium deposits in the joint and possibly elsewhere.

Running subjects the shin bone to an awful beating. The frequent upshot is an affliction many runners have experienced, carelessly called shin splints. Not unlike the common cold, shin splints are a general discomfort in the shin area from inflammation, injury, or stress to the bone or muscles.

Shin splints can be attributed to a number of factors: structural deficiency (low bone density, crooked bones); bad technique (landing on the foot improperly); weak ankle joint (inability to dissipate and control the trauma of contact); tissue damage (tears and/or inflammation in the sheath that surrounds muscles or attaches to the bone); inadvisable running surfaces (too hard, too soft, irregular); overuse syndrome (too much, too soon); and improper footwear. Of these, shoes are probably the most common culprit, the overuse syndrome probably the second most common.

Shin splints are a widespread ailment, but no one seems to have found a cure. To diminish the chance of shin splints, strengthen your first line of defense—your foot and ankle joint; avoid shoes that negatively impact on the foot and Achilles tendon; do not go beyond your fitness level.

To the rear of the shin bone is the calf muscle. It is attached to the Achilles tendon, and is essentially an extension of it. A very strong muscle, it helps to absorb shock, insure flexibility, and stabilize the lower leg. A healthy Achilles tendon usually means a healthy calf muscle.

One of the most complicated areas of the body is the knee joint, where the shin bone and thigh bone meet. Basically its design is that of a simple hinge joint. Bad running technique, such as low heel recovery, forces this joint to act not only as a hinge, however, but also as a swivel. The knee joint was not made to swivel. The tendons and ligaments that hold it in line are not all that strong, and when they are forced to swivel, the unnatural torque and twisting stretches and inflames them.

In response to this inflammation, the body may secrete too little or too much lubricating fluid in the joint area. When there is not enough fluid, the cartilage—which is the covering on the top of the shin bone and on the bottom of the thigh bone—dries out, and the resulting friction causes the tissue in the area to deteriorate. When the joint is swollen from too much fluid, the attendant stiffness and rubbing cause more inflammation compounding the problem and this, in turn, results in the secretion of even more fluids.

Just at push-off, the knee should be aligned with the upper and lower leg as well as with the foot. When the kneecap is misaligned, friction builds up under the cap and along the edges of the groove. It is a condition that can be very painful. Orthotics are often prescribed for this problem, but healthy feet and better running form should cure the problem—unless serious damage has already been done. When the leg is recovered with the heel close to the buttocks, the knee becomes the leading edge. Given enough inertia from the recovery movement of the leg, the knee should swing up to a bit lower than waist level. As this is happening, the heel begins to drop down from under the buttock while the lower leg swings down from the knee joint. When the outside edge of the foot touches the ground again, you have completed one stride cycle (touchdown, support, push off, and recovery).

While the lower leg was moving through the stride cycle, the thigh muscles were put into action. This strong set of muscles on the front of the thigh bone are instrumental in almost all phases of the stride. They help the leg to push down and off the running surface, to bend under the body, and to bring it forward. During touch-down, the thigh muscles also absorb a great deal of shock and help stabilize the leg.

Behind the thigh bone is the hamstring, a group of muscles paid little attention by distance runners. The basic function of the hamstring is to complement the work that the thigh muscles perform as the leg travels through the stride cycles.

A straight line drive of the knee in relationship to the foot and hip is very important in preventing joint injury and wear.

The two muscle groups, not unlike most muscles, work in tandem; they balance each other, insuring efficiency and safety. Yet most distance runners develop their calf and thigh muscles and neglect their hamstring and buttock muscles, which are needed for speed. This neglect is due to the mistaken notion that the ratio between the thigh and the hamstring muscles should be 60:40. Which is to say that if the thigh group can handle sixty pounds, then the hamstring group should be able to handle forty. Because of this imbalance, healthy thigh muscles overwhelm the less-developed hamstring muscles, damaging them, especially when there is call for speed.

Valery Borzov, the great Russian sprinter who won the 1972 Olympic gold medal in the 100 and 200, was a great believer in developing the hamstring. The hamstring, he told me, needed to be at least as strong as the thigh muscle for optimal results in both distance and speed running. It's a point I agree with completely.

To strengthen the hamstring, the hamstring curl is the best exercise.

Another important part of the body involved in the stride cycle is the hip joint. Its function is to anchor the head of the thigh bone in a socket that will allow for the greatest amount of controlled movement. As with the hamstring, this joint is often overlooked until an injury occurs. If it is too tight, the range of the leg's motion will be restricted. If it is too loose, the leg will have too much lateral movement and instability.

The hip joint should be made strong yet should also remain extremely flexible. Hip flexes, hip extensions and front and back squats work to this end. This delicate balance between strength and freedom is essential to good running.

One of the most critical areas of concern in efficient and healthy running is the extreme lower back. Much of the blood supply and nerves that serve the legs pass through the lower back, so an unhealthy lower back impedes their functions.

Tightness, misalignment, or imbalance among muscles in this area can cause major injuries lower in the body. Sciatic problems that cause pain and spasms in the legs, for instance, can often be traced to problems in the lower back.

The lower back area needs regular attention to keep it in shape. Front and back sit-ups help build strength while stretching exercises help increase flexibility. With strength and flexibility in the lower back area, the legs can achieve a full range of motion.

The upper torso is very critical because it contains two of the most vital organs in running—the heart and lungs. If the chest, shoulders, and back are taut, the lungs are not able to inhale and hold their optimal amount of oxygen. Thus, not only is there less oxygen available to fire or energize muscles, but some of that precious little oxygen is appropriated by the tightening muscles which caused the constriction of the lung area in the first place. The result is premature oxygen debt, which is the cause of fatigue.

The best way to reduce upper torso tightness is to keep the lower jaw loose and relaxed. Clenching your teeth cuts down the volume of oxygen you can inhale through your mouth and creates added tension in the upper torso. The effect is a tight upper back that arches rather than leans, which, as explained earlier, is the best position for running.

Stride length and cadence, while there are some who contend otherwise, are directly connected to arm swing. Arms act as a kind of metronome for legs, and the carriage and movement of the arm bear a direct relationship to a runner's style and performance. If a runner has a quick cadence, there will be a corresponding cadence in the movement of the arms. Likewise, if a runner has a long stride length, there will be a longer swing of the arms. (Serious runners will tell you that when they want to change speeds or direction, they do so by initiating a corresponding arm action.)

For best arm action, the shoulders should be as relaxed and

A good straight arm swing is very important to help dampen rotation. Elbows pulled directly behind you help maintain the preferred form.

Arms swung across the body cause rotation and needless wear and tear on joints and lower back.

as flat and square as possible. Very often, runners hunch their shoulders in an effort to pick up their arms, so as not to hamper speed. But what hunching does is to shorten stride length and cause a general tightening in the upper torso and back—which in turn reduces the amount of oxygen you can inhale.

With a bend at the elbows, the arms should be allowed to hang naturally in the shoulder joint. Hands should be relaxed, not clenched. Although many people advocate having the thumb and index fingers touching each other, I have found that the most effective way to maintain relaxation is to run with limp wrists, with the palms facing down.

Arms coordinate tempo, maintain balance, and negate the natural rotary action of the body. For the most effective arm swing, pull the arm back, as if elbowing someone behind you, relax, then let gravity pull the arm down and forward. If the arms swing in a straight line, they dampen the stress caused by the torque and grinding actions involved in running. If, however, the arms swivel, they actually increase the rotary motion and stress, which can lead to injuries in the lower back, the hips, the knees, and the feet. Proper arm swing can reduce your chances of unnecessary effort, tension, fatigue, and injuries.

4

The Essence of Speed Training

As far back as 1971, as the running boom was taking hold, I began to take issue with the prevailing training philosophy in running—LSD, or long slow distance. Running magazines were delighted to publish my criticisms of LSD, because the controversy was always good for heated rebuttals from LSD fanatics. My feeling then was, and still is, that long slow distance training will enable you to run long and slow and nothing more. It will not make you competitive. But it will make a great deal of money for running shoe manufacturers and people who treat running injuries.

The body adapts to what it is made to do most often. If it is commanded to run long and slow, given enough time to adapt, it will become very good at running long, assuming it is asked to do so slowly. These long slow runs, of course, do some good. Most significantly, they aid in cardiovascular fitness. In too many instances, however, athletes confuse cardiovascular fitness with race fitness.

Starting from rock bottom, or near rock bottom, any training will produce early improvements. Because of the increased conditioning levels, your times will get faster over given distances. The problem is that your improvements will cease prematurely, and you will reach a plateau way short of your ultimate potential. Runners who reach this plateau, with only LSD as a guide, tend simply to increase their mileage. If a few miles are good, the thinking goes, then a lot of miles must be a lot better. In truth, the added mileage only subjects you to frustration and injury. The megamileage encouraged by LSD training requires the use of increasingly more sophisticated (and expensive) shoes. Such shoes are necessary to address the injuries sustained from excessive foot exertion, from ill-designed shoes, from bad running technique—or some combination of the above. As runners fixate upon running more and more miles, they end up paying the cost physically as well as financially.

Fifteen years ago, my notions about less mileage and more attention to speed and technique were ridiculed and rejected. I was dismissed as a sprint coach who was unqualified to pass judgment on what was good for distance runners. Over the years, though, there has been a general disillusionment with LSD. I'm gratified to note that views have shifted to the "new" idea that intelligent training in speed, even for distance runners, is essential.

The biggest problem with LSD is not what it represents as a training philosophy. As a training and low-effort conditioning concept, LSD is, in fact, very sound. It was supposed to allow sedentary, out-of-shape, noncompetitive people to get back some semblance of fitness and muscle tone, with minimal effort and risk. It was never meant to be the centerpiece of a serious training philosophy for competitive runners; it was meant for joggers. But speed and distance runners alike embraced the training philosophy, few taking the time to understand what LSD was intended to do. What racers must understand when planning their training is that in order to run fast and race competitively, speed must be emphasized. Strength, technique, and desire, are obviously necessary, but these qualities must be combined with what I call speed training.

Speed is an essential element in endurance as well. In too many instances, athletes have not properly understood the real meaning of endurance—which, simply stated, is the ability to run a given distance at a certain speed. Consider, however, if it takes one runner five hours to complete a marathon, while it takes another three hours, who has more endurance? By definition, it is the slower runner, because he has "endured" longer, but when viewed in this light, the virtue of endurance alone becomes suspect. The slower runner in this case has more endurance—but at a much slower speed.

Slow marathon runners rely on aerobic-type training, but such training alone is not enough for a runner who wishes to maximize his or her potential. Anaerobic work is also necessary to improve the cardiovascular system and to better running times.

In a marathon, an athlete runs at his or her endurance level. This speed is usually well below the maximum speed an athlete can handle, which means that the speed is well within the comfort and tolerance zone of the runner. In speed training, an athlete increases his basic leg turnover rate with the result that he reaches a comfort zone that is faster than before. In order to run longer distances, he needs to increase his aerobic capacity, his oxygen transportation and absorption. But in order to run both longer and faster effectively, he must increase his basic leg turnover rate as well as distance.

Speed training, like LSD, can lead to abuse and injury unless properly understood. My tendency to gloat over the recognition of the importance of speed in training is tempered with the fear that speed training will become the prevailing "commonly accepted" training fad. There are benefits and rewards it can bring, but the basic concepts of speed training must first be fully appreciated.

The runner must first determine what he or she is seeking. Too many people con themselves into the idea that running for running's sake is their goal. This is true in very few cases. Most people gauge the success of their running against some sort of measurable standard, such as how many miles they can run in a given time frame, or how fast they can run over a given distance. This is not running for the sake of running. This is competitive running.

Running for the sake of running certainly has its pleasures. The activity itself provides satisfaction, not how long it takes or how fast you go. If you simply enjoy the physical activity associated with running, then LSD is unquestionably the best philosophy for you. However, as soon as running per se is not enough and the need for something more is present, then you are a competitive runner, and LSD is no longer a sound primary training philosophy. Once you have determined the nature of your quest in running, the type of training philosophy naturally follows.

My role as a varsity coach is to coach competitive runners. My success or failure depends on how well my athletes race. Success for me is not based so much upon whether or not my athlete wins, but upon how well I have prepared that athlete to do his or her best under the existing circumstances.

My approach to training athletes to become faster is based on the following principles.

1. As long as success is based upon how little time is involved in running any distance, then speed is the central and most integral element in training.
2. Through proper training, speed, like endurance, can be increased.
3. Given enough time, the body will adapt to whatever stress or demands are placed on it. The more specific the demands, the more effective the results.
4. No runner can endure very long at near maximum speed.
5. Given a certain cardiovascular level, the better the basic speed, the greater the capacity for endurance and speed endurance.

My explanation of speed training here is not to present the reader with a workout program to be followed blindly. Instead it is to provide a fundamental understanding of what needs to be done so that each runner will be able to devise a personalized program that is based upon specific needs and conditions. Thus, as the athlete matures, or the conditioning level changes, so may the program.

The competitive athlete's goal should be to increase his or her "comfort zone" or cruise pace, which is the speed at which the athlete is able to race comfortably. By training much faster than this cruise pace, the body learns to handle greater speed, and the cruise pace can be faster as the athlete becomes faster.

Athletes with any level of ability must understand that there are only four basic types of workouts.

1. Absolute speed: Here you turn over your legs as fast and as often as you can. This develops your absolute speed reservoir. This workout is not designed to make everyone into a sprinter; it is used to enhance your leg turnover rate.
2. Endurance: This is the basic concept used in long slow distance training. The purpose of this workout is to build up the capillary pads in your muscles and to help you develop better circulation. You should run at least an hour at a very slow speed. This helps to increase your ability to handle the oxygen intake so that you can run as long as possible before going into oxygen debt.
3. Speed endurance: This workout builds up the body's ability to run at target times over target distances with a certain amount of debt present. You run, for example, a target distance, take a short recovery, then repeat the same distance or another target distance.
4. Rest and recovery: You do very little in this stage as you allow your body to recover and repair itself.

For competitors, much of speed training translates into anaerobic training. Assuming a degree of aerobic development in a runner, speed training introduces muscles to anaerobic stress that can be expected in a race: To wait until well into training to do this is a recipe for disappointment and injury.

The reason that speed is primary in any training equation is because speed is not only necessary for success, it is also knowable. For example, you can know how to set your "race pace" to be well within your comfort zone.

Now the speed training program for both sprinter and distance runner is based upon the premise, noted earlier, that no one can run at maximum speed for any significant distance during a race. Both sprinter and distance runner run at a speed that is below their maximum but is fast enough to keep up with the prevailing race pace or with their own target race pace. What a runner wants, then, is to have the highest comfortable race pace. The higher the comfortable race pace, the better the Winning Edge.

A sprinter can feel fairly comfortable—and competitive—with the race pace at approximately 90 to 95 percent of maximum turnover speed. For the distance runner, the race pace has to be closer to 65 percent of maximum turnover speed. Of course, there are variances. Some distance runners can sustain a pace of nearly 70 to 75 percent of maximum turnover speed, while others only somewhere in the 60 percent range. Regardless of what the percentage is, the runner must be trained so that the race pace is within his or her comfort zone. Once the faster than race pace is sustained for a number of repetitions in training, the athlete can comfortably know that he or she has the speed necessary to run the target time. If that target time cannot be met, in a race where the athlete has given a good competitive effort, then there is an aerobic deficiency: More oxygen efficiency is needed to facilitate the metabolic process, thus LSD is in order.

Like the sprinter, the distance runner must pay special attention to strength, flexibility, and speed enhancement. Both sprinters and distance runners should be aware that a race is usually won—or time goals met—over the last 25 percent of the race and very rarely in the early segments. For marathon runners, that means training for the stresses that occur over the last five to seven miles.

Unless trained to respond to such stresses, however, muscles that have been conditioned and have adapted to the unique concerns of slow running will be reluctant to work at a pace that is much quicker. While the rest of the body may be fit and ready to blast, the neglected muscles will not have developed the necessary tolerance to handle this new demand.

The converse is true in terms of the biochemistry engaged in running as well. In aerobic activity—long slow distance running—oxygen is the primary energy source for the body. In anaerobic activity—the short, intense efforts of the body—the primary energy source is glycogen. Muscles have a glycogen supply of about 13 to 18 seconds. In training, the body learns to cultivate this energy source and, when there is need for speed, to depend upon it.

For speed endurance, the primary energy source is lactic acid. The by-product of muscle metabolism, lactic acid becomes valuable when the body finds itself in activity beyond aerobic capacity and when the supply of glycogen has been consumed. Lactic acid, however, is not an energy source the body particularly likes; it would rather slow down and go back to using oxygen instead. If the aim is not to slow down, then lactic acid is necessary—especially in any race over one hundred meters. What training does is to adapt the body to using lactic acid.

Developing aerobic and anaerobic fitness *concurrently* is therefore critical. Opportunity for injury is diminished, and speed, when necessary, can be called upon. Note, though, that any anaerobic stress loading—that is, a quickening of the race pace—must be done gradually and the body must be given proper time to adjust incrementally.

Here is where I am at odds with most coaches. A "base" or "background" of aerobic training should be developed first, they believe, then, in the "peaking period," when the most important meets of the year are to take place, speed training is introduced. The problem that I have with this method is that no one can predict, within a couple of hundred training miles, how much base is needed to run a certain time for a certain distance. On the other hand, I can predict, within a few seconds, how much training speed is required to run a certain distance in a certain time.

This is the most efficient and most scientific way to establish what elements of training are required to meet a given goal. Weeks and months can be wasted in developing a base that was already in place. Since there is no measurable way to know how much base is actually present, then the coach and athlete subscribing to this training method are playing athletic blindman's bluff.

But in speed training, the prescriptions are more forthright. If, for example, you have established your "speed base," but still cannot run the desired time, you know the deficiency is aerobic. You should simply increase your mileage on your endurance runs, perhaps up to an hour and a half. If on the other hand, you are running your speed at target times and your endurance runs are long enough but your overall performance isn't good enough, the deficiency is anaerobic. You should focus on speed/endurance training by running target distances in times better than race pace with a short recovery. For a five-minute mile, you should run between four and eight 440s at a speed of 65 to 70 seconds with a 220 jog or 110 walk. If this does not work, then probably the culprit is burnout, and more rest and recovery is the answer.

* * *

The importance of rest and recovery cannot be overemphasized. In training, this period should be viewed in terms of the basic, operative mechanism of the "overcompensation syndrome." Overcompensation is the mind's way of defending and protecting the body against the shock and trauma of stress.

When an athlete who is a 10 on a scale of 100 in terms of fitness level starts to train, his system is shocked into working at a level beyond his present fitness. Minor damage is done to parts of the body—to muscle fibers, connective tissue, joints, and the skeletal system. Body and mind immediately respond to the alarm and shock caused by the overload. During the interval between the stress periods, natural healing substances and anti-inflammatory agents are rushed to the damaged areas of the body. As a result, the mind prepares the body to withstand an even greater shock the next time a similar stress is induced. As more stress is incrementally introduced to the body, the fitness level gradually rises to approach 100. This is the overcompensation syndrome.

It is one of the basic tenets of good training. During the rest and recovery phase your body heals itself, and the overcompensation syndrome kicks in. If your body does not have sufficient rest and recovery, then you will not make progress in your training.

The notion that it is beneficial to work hard at every training session is obviously fallacious. Overzealous or ignorant coaches and athletes who feel that "without pain there can be no gain" are terribly misguided. Just as running long slow distance is great training for running long and slow, training with pain is great only for learning to run with pain, and to create more pain. This is not intelligent training.

The idea of training is to allow the athlete to excel without extreme amounts of pain. Most great races I have witnessed have been "effortless," according to the athletes themselves. Courageous efforts with great pain may be courageous, but they rarely produce records. They are mostly an opportunity for an athlete to show how much guts he or she has. Infinitely better would be if that same gutsy athlete had trained so that he or she could have had a healthy success.

Rest and recovery should be an integral part of your training. Every work session has to be followed by a recovery session of commensurate intensity. The choice is yours. Either you plan a rest phase in your training program, or the rest phase will plan itself—as a time for injury recovery. Like the man in the commercial says, "You can pay me now or you can pay me later." You should "pay as you go." Dick Brown, the brilliant former coach of Mary Slaney, states it best for middle and long distance runners. With Mary, he was concerned not with her mileage per week but her mileage over the year.

Any rational training program is based on the idea that stress tears down the body while rest restores it. But not only does rest restore, it restores to a higher level than the original level.

Finally, a runner needs to guard against the "overuse syndrome." According to Dr. Stan James, one of the foremost orthopedic surgeons in the country, the overuse syndrome is responsible for the great majority of running injuries he has treated. It is a problem to which runners seem particularly predisposed—a problem of not knowing when to stop. The urge to overdo, to prolong the exercise compulsively and addictively, is almost always present.

It is natural for the runner to respond positively to moderate exercise. The body feels good—in large part because, in exercise, the body secretes a series of painkillers, anti-inflammatory agents, and endorphins that combine to produce a kind of "high." And the body wishes to reproduce this sensation. As running would seem to be a healthy, natural high, the tendency is, as with a recreational drug, to overuse, to abuse.

The runner does not, however, as with a recreational drug,

have to do more to get the same high as before. As a matter of fact, when he overdoes it, the body's natural drugstore stops dispensing the drugs in sufficient quantity to satisfy psychological needs. A simple backing off of effort will allow the body to revitalize and resupply the store, enough to keep the runner happily running right along.

The key here is to understand the limits and limitations of exercise. If you get good biofeedback from a certain quantity and quality of work, then simply try to maintain that level of intensity, rather than radically increasing it to the point of injury. In moderation the body will supply enough of the healing and rehabilitation substances necessary to keep the machinery in good repair and ready to run. If you are running above thirty miles a week, then simply run until you reach your optimum point and don't go over that limit. After a while you will sense a natural need to increase your mileage, simply do so gradually until the high returns and maintain that level. Discipline and control over effort are essential to good health and well-being in running. Compulsive running will only negate the positive.

5

The Basic Training Program

Speed training incorporates the four essential elements of training—speed, endurance, speed endurance, and rest and recovery. (Form and technique as well as strength training are no less important and are discussed in detail in other chapters.)

If you are a recreational jogger, please note that this program assumes a certain level of fitness that may exceed your own: you should consult a physician before undertaking this strenuous physical activity.

If we assume that all races are on Saturday, Sunday is a day of active rest and recovery. This means an easy run of 45 minutes to an hour. Your pulse should not rise above 160–170.

Monday is speed day. This would involve between 12 to 24 110-yard sprints, depending on your fitness. There would be a 330-yard recovery jog between each sprint.

Tuesday is speed endurance day. You would run say, six 880 or one-mile repeats with a 90-second recovery. The number of repeats and target times would vary depending on circumstances.

Wednesday is a day of active rest. You should jog an easy 30- to 45-minute run; or you could put in the time bicycling or swimming if you want to get off the track.

Thursday is endurance or peripheral run day. This is a true aerobic run of up to one and one half hours. The purpose here is to sustain activity—to relax and invigorate. There should be a minimum of stress and no fatigue.

Friday is another day of active rest with an easy run of 45 minutes or more.

Saturday is race day. If Saturday's race is critical and near the end of a training cycle, it would be preceded by two days of rest instead of one.

It is my feeling that a runner can peak after eight to twelve weeks of training. Since school terms at Stanford are ten weeks and NCAA national championships seem to fall at the end of each term, we work on a ten-week cycle. Supposing that an athlete wants to ready himself or herself in a like period of time, here is a program to follow:

WEEK ONE

Monday—Speed. 880 and longer distance runners would run 12–16 110 yards with a 330 recovery jog at 70 percent maximum turnover rate. Sprinters would run 4–8 110s at 80 percent with a 330 recovery.

Tuesday—Speed endurance. Distance runners should run 4–6 440s or 880s or miles at 75–80 percent with 90-second recovery jogs. Sprinters should run 3–6 330s, 440s, or 500s at 65–70 percent with 2-minute recoveries.

Wednesday—Active rest and recovery. All runners should do an easy run of 45 minutes.

Thursday—Endurance. Distance runners should do a run of up to 1 hour. Sprinters should run for 30 to 40 minutes.

Friday—Rest and recovery. All runners should do an easy run of 45 minutes.

Saturday—Endurance or rest and recovery. Distance runners should run for an hour with pulse getting no higher than 160–170. Sprinters should not run.

Sunday—Optional. You may either run or rest.

WEEK TWO

Follow the same training as Week One, but include two days of strength training. Do longer runs; and do runs of an intensity between sprint and LSD, with short recovery. Remember to pay special attention to form and technique training as well.

WEEK THREE

Basically the same as Week One and Two, with a third day of strength training added. Runners have the option of starting morning runs—either this week or the next.

WEEK FOUR

Monday. Distance runners should run 16–24 110 yards with a 330 recovery jog. The 110s are done at 85 percent of maximum turnover rate for the middle eight laps. The first 8 are done at 70 percent and the last 8 at 75 percent. Sprinters should run 8–12 110s all at 85 percent.

Tuesday. Runners 5000, 10,000, and up should run 6–8 mile repeats at 75 percent with a 440 recovery jog. Runners 1500–3000 should run 6–8 880 repeats at 75 percent with a 440 recovery jog. Sprinters should run 3–4 330s at 75 percent with a 440 recovery jog.

Pictured here is excellent body position and overall technique. Note the foot is directly under body. The body is relaxed and somewhat compressed, absorbing shock and readying itself for a spring upward and forward. Also note the forward lean of the body, the high heel recovery, and general attitude of relaxation and control.

Wednesday. Active rest day: all runners should do an easy 45-minute run.

Thursday. All runners should do a peripheral or endurance run of 1½ hours. Sprinters should begin work on skills such as blocks and baton passes.

Friday. For distance runners, an active rest day: 45-minute run followed by 15–30 minutes of formwork. Sprinters have the day off.

Saturday. All runners except sprinters should do a peripheral or endurance run of 1½–1¾ hours.

Sunday. All runners have the option of either resting or running.

WEEK FIVE

Monday. Runners 5000 and up should run 6–8 repeat miles at 75 percent with a 220 recovery jog. Runners 1500–3000 should run 6–8 800s at 80 percent with a 440 recovery. All 800 runners should run 6–8 440s at 80 percent with a 660 recovery. Sprinters should run four 40 meters, four 60 meters, and four 100 meters at 85 percent.

Tuesday. Distance runners should run twenty-four 110 yards, 8 at 75 percent, 8 at 90 percent, 8 at 70 percent. Sprinters should do skill work.

Wednesday. Distance runners should run for 45 minutes, then do an easy 30 minutes of form work. Sprinters should run four 220s at 80 percent with full recovery.

Thursday. Distance runners should run an endurance run of 1½ hours. Sprinters should do skill work.

Friday. Distance runners have a day of active rest. Sprinters have the day off.

Saturday. Distance runners should run trial races, focusing on their target time for the last 25 percent of the distance run, the toughest and most crucial part of the race. During the first 75 percent of the run, they should run at a moderate, relaxed pace. Sprinters rest.

Sunday. All runners have the option to rest or to run—but for no more than, say, 40 percent the normal length of time.

You should keep in mind that this entire training program is based upon the idea that your race pace should be within your comfort zone. Maximum exertion should only take place over the last 25 percent of the race. Since most races are won over this stretch, the sooner the runner is confident of his or her ability during this segment the better. In terms of time, the goal is to run the last 25 percent of a race about 5 to 10 percent faster than the anticipated race pace. For example, if you want to run a 4:00-minute mile, then the last quarter mile should be run within 57 or 55 seconds or better. Unless you reach this time, it is unlikely that you have enough speed for a 4:00 mile.

Once you have met the target time for the last 25 percent during your trial race, you can shift your focus to endurance or speed endurance. At this point, you can close the rest interval between repetitions or add more repetitions, depending on your strengths and weaknesses. If you need more overall aerobic strength, then you should add more repetitions. If you lack brute strength, then you should either run faster with the same rest intervals or run the same repetitions with shorter rest intervals.

How can you gauge your strengths and weaknesses?

One of the simplest diagnostic tools to check your progress is the pulse rate. In matters of fitness, the heart rarely lies. Comparing your running pulse to your resting pulse can help you determine how aerobically fit you are. You should take your pulse immediately after the race, then three more times—two minutes later, five minutes after that, and then 10 minutes later.

If your pulse drops radically and approaches your resting rate, then aerobic and cardiovascular conditioning is not your problem; you need instead to work more on speed endurance training. Your resting pulse is the average of your pulse first thing in the morning and before bedtime at night. If your pulse rate is 25 percent or more than your normal resting rate, then you should reduce your workload by the same percentage as the pulse increase.

Another diagnostic tool is the 110-yard sprint. If over the course of a week your times get slower and you have an elevated pulse rate and/or a weight loss, then you have troubles. These are signs of overtraining, injury, illness, or burnout. You should stop or back off radically.

Now you're ready for week six. Depending on the results of week five, we would typically back off and see if we can generate a mid-phase peak.

WEEK SIX

Monday. Distance runners 5000 and up should run 3-mile repeats at 90 percent with 2-minute recovery jogs. Runners 1500-3000 should run four 880s at 90 percent with 2-minute recovery jogs. All 800 athletes should do sixteen 220 recovery jogs. Sprinters should run trial races of 40, 60, or 100 meters.

Tuesday. Distance runners should do twenty-four 110 yards at 80 percent with a 330 recovery jog. Sprinters should do skill work.

Wednesday. Distance runners should do a rest and recovery run of 30 minutes with 30 minutes of form and technique work. Sprinters should do four 40s, four 60s, and four 100s.

Thursday. Distance runners have an optional day during which they should do light work that they enjoy. Sprinters should do block work with starts for 15 yards, and finish with an easy 400.

Friday. All runners should rest and recover.

Saturday. All runners should do race or time trials.

Sunday. Peripheral or endurance run for distance runners. Sprinters take the day off.

The next four weeks involve fine tuning. By now, a runner should have established both an aerobic and anaerobic base, and his or her strengths and weaknesses should now be evident. If you have followed this program, then you can correct your identifiable deficiencies over the next four weeks. (At this point, the coach and the athlete would have an in-depth discussion about progress of the training.)

If the program has been successfully followed, then there may be a need for only small or subtle changes in the training. Usually the athlete has the best feel in these areas. If things are going well, then the need for change is minimal. (Only the coach/athlete can make this determination.)

Many of the athletes that I have coached using this training program have had considerable success. These included such national champions as Steve Williams, for his indoor 60-yard and outdoor 100-meter championships, and Dr. Kim Schnurpfeil for her 10,000 meters, winning both the NCAA and TAC track championships at this distance in the same year. The first to ever do so. This training program works regardless of your gender or distance. A crucial part of this program is that, in addition to the four critical areas of physical training, speed training has been implemented early. Very few programs acknowledge the need for an anaerobic as well as an aerobic base.

The key concept of this program—in fact of the Winning Edge itself—is that of peaking. I guess I am going to shock a great many coaches and athletes by stating that, while there may be a peaking period at the times of important races, there is really no such thing as peaking. Peaking is a figment of the imagination.

Reaching a peak simply means doing the best job you can under the circumstances. You can do that every day. On some days, that means running very hard or very long. On other days, that means just jogging easy. On other days, it means doing nothing at all. As you progressively train, you progressively perform better. Every day can be an improvement over the previous day, every day should mark progress. Accordingly, each day can be a peak.

In race conditions, circumstances will of course vary, but because you are prepared to peak no matter what, you will have the Winning Edge.

6

OMNIBUS DRILLS AND EXERCISES

Designed for basic and supplemental strength training, drills and exercises are an important part of any runner's workout. One of the drawbacks of drills, however, is that many people get carried away with them. Drills are meant to supplement regular training, not replace it. There is no drill that is as good as doing the actual physical activity in question.

The following drills may be performed prior to workouts or during stretching sessions at any time during the day.

THE FOOT, INCLUDING CALF MUSCLES AND SOLEUS MUSCLES

1. Step drills. These are done barefoot. Walk in a very deliberate manner, accenting the walking movement throughout the entire range of motion of the foot. Your heel touches first, the rest of the foot comes to rest flat, and then roll up onto the very tip of the big toe very slowly—so as to work the muscles, tendons, and ligaments throughout the entire foot. Do this one step at a time, taking the time to be precise with each step. It is best to do this drill on a grass field, on a beach, or on a carpeted surface.

2. Toe raisers. Place the front half of your foot on a slightly raised surface, like a 2 × 4. Your heel should start out lower than the ball of your foot. Very slowly raise your heel up until you are balanced as high on your toes as possible. Repeat this as many times as seems desirable. You may, if you wish, do this exercise with extra weights on your shoulders.

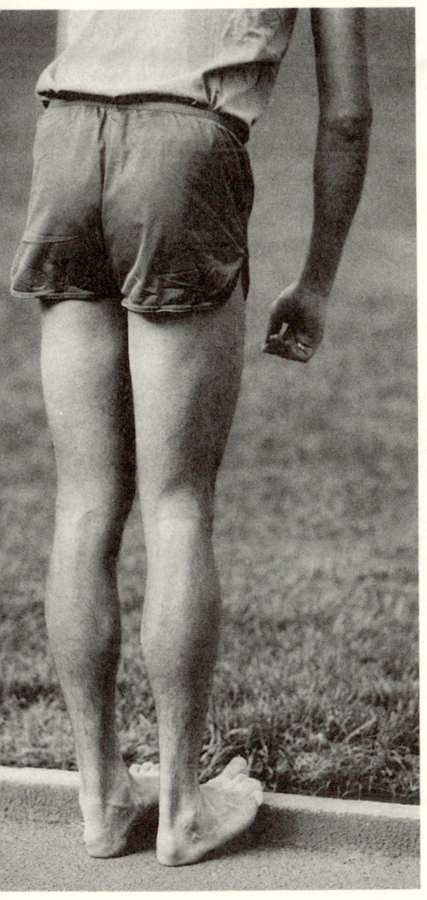

This is an excellent exercise for foot and lower leg strength and flexibility.

3. Stair drills. Simply walk very slowly with a pronounced tempo up stairs, bleachers, or anything with graduated increments. Make sure that on each stair you roll as high up on your toes as possible. Again, you can do this exercise with weights on your shoulders.

This is the step drill against resistance. In this case stadium stairs are used, but it can be done on stairs in the home as well.

4. Toe curls. Spread a towel or sheet on the floor. Using only your toes, grip the fabric and pull it back. This can be done while you are sitting or standing, while you are reading, or while you are watching television.

THE THIGH MUSCLES

1. Step downers. With or without weight on your shoulders, simply walk very slowly down stairs, bleachers, or any other graduated incline. On the way down, allow your hips to drop as low as possible, almost to a sitting position.

2. Depth jumps. Simply jump up on a box or platform, then jump back down onto the ground, and then back up on the box. Do so as quickly as you can, barely allowing yourself to come to rest either on the box or on the ground. You can also line up several boxes or platforms and jump from one to the ground, immediately back up onto the next box, immediately back down to the ground, and so on. In addition to working the thighs, this exercise will also help develop foot, calf, and ankle muscles.

THE HAMSTRING MUSCLES

These exercises are important for speed and endurance training.

1. Hamstring curls. In any weight-lifting facility, you will find a hamstring curl machine. Attach the weight to your ankles, and pull your lower legs up toward your buttocks using your hamstring and buttocks muscles. The closer you can get your heels to your buttocks the better. This is a very dangerous exercise, however, so it should be attempted with caution. At the least indication of cramping in the hamstring, stop immediately.

2. Back squats. Squats are a very dangerous lift, especially if you lack the proper technique. I would not normally advocate squats, but if a hamstring curl machine is not available, then this is an alternative. Holding a barbell or any other type of light weight that is no more than 25 percent of your total body weight to start, very slowly move from a standing position to a squat position and then back up again. Take special care to keep the weight steady and your back straight. Also, try to hold the weight near the midline of the body.

3. Isometric hamstring curls. Lying on your stomach, hook your heels under a heavy chair, couch, table, or anything else that won't move, and simply pull against the object using your hamstring muscles. Do this for a minute with a minute recovery in between each curl. Another variation is to do the same exercise with someone holding your heels down. You can also anchor your heels and do reverse sit-ups by using the muscles in your buttocks and hamstring, and raising your chest off the floor. *If you have lower back problems, do not attempt this exercise.*

THE LOWER BACK

When you run, your lower back is subjected to not only extra weight but also to extra torque. The following exercises will help strengthen your lower back to withstand the extra stresses of compression and rotation caused by running.

1. Reverse incline reclining. Simply lie down on an incline board with your feet above your head. Gravity should slowly and gently tug down on your torso, relieving the pressure on your lower back. The more relaxed you are, the more you will benefit from this exercise.

2. Trunk rotations. Stand erect, clasp your hands behind your head, and rotate your lower body as far as possible, to your right and then to your left. A variation of this is to clasp your hands behind your head, rotate down toward your knees, and try to touch your knees with your elbows. This exercise helps stretch the muscles in your lower back.

THE ARM MUSCLES

All too often, there is an imbalance between the strength of the arms and the strength of the legs. The following exercises will help to develop and strengthen the muscles in your arms:

1. Hand weights. Simply run or jog with weights in your hands. Try to run with as natural an arm swing as possible. If this cannot be done, then the weights are too heavy.

2. Wrist curls. Extend your hands out over the edge of a supporting platform. Place the weight in your hands and curl your hands toward your body.

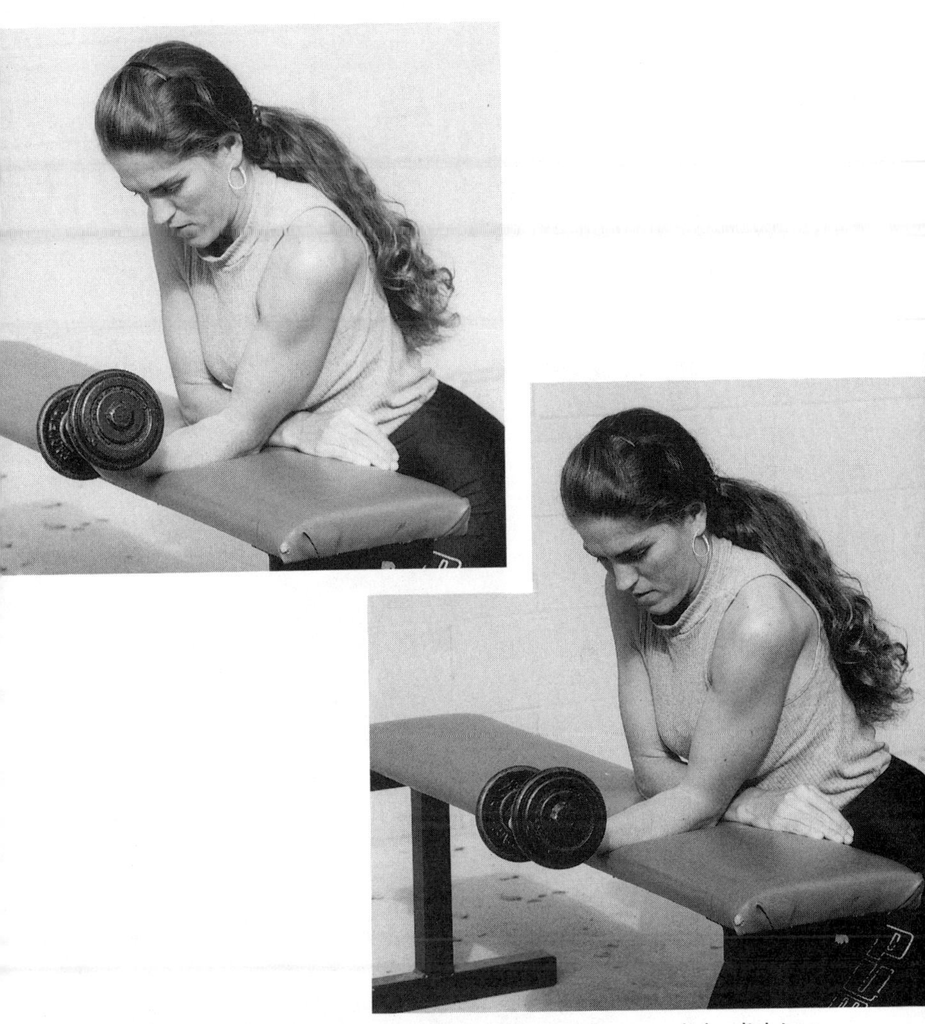

Strengthening the forearm area is very important because it is vital to a strong arm swing while keeping shoulders relaxed.

3. Arm curls. With the weight in your hand, simply curl your arm toward the shoulder, bending at the elbow joint.

Arm curls are very important in order to strengthen the lower arm area to help with a strong and smooth arm swing.

GENERAL SUPPLEMENTARY EXERCISES

1. Butt Kickers. Run in place and try to kick your heels high enough to touch your buttocks with each upward swing. Once you have mastered this while running in place, then try doing it while running 50 to 100 meters several times. This increases flexibility in your thighs and helps you get into the habit of a high heel recovery while running.

2. Skip drills. This is a movement just like that used in hopscotch. First try skipping for height. Then try skipping for distance. Then try skipping for speed.

3. Losing the fear of falling. Using a slight incline, practice running down the incline with an exaggerated body lean. This will help you overcome your natural fear of falling. It also gives you added practice for running with a proper body lean.

4. Tumbling. This is perhaps one of the most important drills for athletes who "naturally" feel awkward. Research has shown that rolling around as a baby is an essential stage of development for your motor skills. So for people who seem to have bypassed that stage, or whose fear of falling diminishes their speed, tumbling will give you confidence. Tumbling can be anything that involves rolling around or being upside down and moving. This can be done on grass, sand, mats, or carpets.

The intensity and frequency of these drills are your own choice based on your needs and strengths. Most training facilities and health spas have someone who can plan a personalized fitness program for you if you need help deciding what is best for you.

My recommended daily stretching exercises that work on critical areas of flexibility. They are particularly good for stretching and developing flexibility in the lower back area. This is critical because a lot of bad habits and techniques originate with lower back stiffness and rigidity.

PUMA

7

DIET AND NUTRITION

Health and general well-being are directly related to diet and nutrition. Your body is potentially no better than what you take in by way of nourishment.

Although many magazines, newspapers, and television shows regularly tout new diets, there is still no definitive diet for an athlete. The situation can be described as a dietetic dialectic. As soon as one diet or food plan is offered and gains recognition, it is supplanted by another one in direct opposition to the basic principles of the first. The result is a jumble of conflicting and confusing information from so-called experts who are only trying to get rich quick.

The solution to the diet dilemma is to rely on basic common sense. No single diet will be the best for everyone because only a personalized, unique diet will be best for each individual. It is my feeling that if you ignore any social or cultural pressures, norms and biases in determining what and how much to eat, your natural instincts will lead you to a balanced diet. A general rule might be to eat as many different-colored foods as you can and to guard against overeating and undereating.

The secret to a good diet is based not so much on good foods, but what foods are good for you. Foods that your body can easily break down into usable substances are more nutritious than "good" foods that your digestive system must struggle with. All too often, health foods are not broken down fast enough to be sufficiently processed by the body. This is often true of vitamins and food supplements that come in capsule or tablet form.

Capsules or tablets are often treated with a protective covering. The body has to eat through this coating before getting to the substance inside. If this coating is something that the body does not handle well, then the benefits of the capsule and tablet can be long gone before they have done any good. Powdered or readily digestible supplements are by far the best form to take.

Water is the only substance that I can categorically suggest as essential and right for any diet. The body is composed of at least 90 percent water, and water is the base ingredient of most of the body's functions. Nutritionally, the runner's best friend is water. This may sound odd, but the fact of the matter is that the importance of water cannot be overemphasized. In addition to helping dissolve nutrients into a usable form, water also acts as the basis for the lubricants that help keep the joints and muscles moving smoothly. Water helps reduce inflammation in the joints, tendons, and ligaments, and it also helps keep the tissues pliable and elastic. In addition, the body uses water-based fluids to keep the body temperature at the proper level. So the common denominator to any diet is to drink a sufficient quantity of water so that the body can function properly.

The eating disorders of anorexia and bulimia are not uncommon among runners. This is particularly the case with women, but not exclusively so; among men the problem is just not as well documented. Whether male or female, runners are easy prey to anorexia and bulimia because there is usually an instant reward for compulsive dieting. The weight loss will almost immediately give the runner better performances. Because there is a temporary favorable weight-to-strength ratio, given a certain fitness level, an underweight runner will be able, for a time, to actually run faster or longer.

Once the runner has been hooked on the first flush of success as a result of losing weight, the desire to lose more weight in order to increase the performance level takes over. Depending upon the mental toughness and basic constitution of the runner, this cycle of weight loss and performance enhancement can go on until the runner starts to lose too much of the tissue carelessly referred to as fat. Now if this fat has been grossly in excess of what is needed for health and wellness, then the loss can be a plus. But when the weight loss goes beyond and impacts negatively on natural body functions, then the runner is courting trouble. Generally speaking, for both women and men, if the proportion of fat to body weight falls below 10 percent, you are in the danger zone. (Women will cease to menstruate when their body fat approaches this low point.) Stop the dieting, and see a doctor immediately.

The body requires a certain amount of fat for reserve and safety. Fatty tissue is basically the body's way of storing up unused energy sources for a rainy day. It is rather ironic to note that distance runners will diet and lose weight, and then before a big race "carbohydrate load"—seeking exactly the kind of energy sources they have lost through dieting. True, too much of a good thing is too much, but a certain amount of reserve is natural, normal, and healthy. When the reserve has been lost, there is nothing left in case of stress or emergency.

If compulsive dieting is not checked, the body will start to burn up lean muscle mass because it does not have the fatty tissue to burn. This is a serious matter. Because there is no reserve when there is the most need, the runner destroys the very tissue required to perform the function of running in the first place. This is a no-win paradox of the greatest magnitude.

Fatty tissue, in addition to holding reserve fuel, provides protection and padding. Inordinate loss of weight will result in loss of the shock-absorbing function that fatty pads give to the feet, lower back, knees, joints, and elsewhere in the body. Opportunity for injury is thus increased. (For a measure of protection, even if you do not overdiet, place a foot-shaped bladder of silicon gel in your shoes; it will act in much the same way as a layer of fatty tissue in the feet, and is very effective.) Especially in women, for whom there is blood loss through menstruation, the pounding and jolting sustained by the feet in particular, and the body in general, while running, result in a significant amount of blood cell loss. For people susceptible to anemia as well, this can prove very dangerous.

Bones are also negatively impacted by excessive weight loss. Bone cells, like blood cells, have a life cycle and must be replenished. Additionally, like blood cells, they can be prematurely damaged by shock. After such shock, the body will attempt to manufacture more bone cells to help harden the skeletal system, but this can only be done if there are proper raw materials present in the body. If there is not the proper intake of foods, the body cannot work to rehabilitate, protect, and strengthen itself.

8

COACH TO COACH: TEACHING THE WINNING EDGE

My advice to coaches is to focus on what you can control. Set on a goal each day and determine, with the athlete, how best to accomplish it. Likewise, the training and conditioning should always be consistent with those goals.

Long-term goals are no less important than the aims of a particular workout. In too many instances, a coach has goals and aspirations for an athlete that are neither clear to nor shared by the athlete. Many times a coach will think of the athlete as having the capability to score at a major meet, whether it be at the high school state meet or at the Olympic trials. All the while, though, the athlete's goal may simply be to get to the meet.

Often, an athlete will grow frustrated and indifferent because of confusion over goals. Burnout is a frequent result. On the other hand, an athlete may have achieved the year's goal in two months instead of the projected twelve months. There is the tendency for the athlete to burn out in this case as well, not because the athlete has been overworked or overtrained, but because he or she reached a goal not shared by the coach.

I once coached, or attempted to coach, a very talented athlete who made tremendous progress up until the middle of the season. After that, his progress stopped and he became lethargic. I could not understand why he was merely treading water. My first thought was that I had burned him out, but given the time frame and work load, I knew that could not be the problem. I checked with his family, teachers, and friends, and learned of no personal problems.

Finally, I asked him what his goals were for that year. He told me. They were the exact times he was running, despite the fact that he had the potential for doing much better. He had set his goals for the year and had accomplished them. He was highly motivated to achieve his original goals, but after that it was all anticlimactic.

The next year we set goals that were more in line with his talent. The problem was that he took his time working to attain them. He was determined not to get caught in the trap I had set for him. Sometimes if you are going to motivate someone, you have to be smarter than the person you are trying to motivate.

The Winning Edge is not always easy to see, especially at first glance. The U.S. Olympic trials and the Olympic Games in 1976 provided me with some very painful experiences which, I'm gratified to note, later produced record Olympic results in 1984.

At the 1976 U.S. Olympic trials, I had two athletes who normally would have made the U.S. Olympic Team. Robin Campbell, who was one of America's premier 400- and 800-meter runners, had been running since she was nine. At age fourteen, she defeated the Russians and, along with Mary Slaney, formed a nucleus of very talented *wunderkinder* during the middle seventies.

Before the U.S. Olympic trials, however, Campbell sustained a bad case of shin splints. This was her first injury, and she did not know just how well she could run with the ailment. As a result of her anxieties, she ran tentatively and did not make the team. Later, though, with even more severe handicaps, she was able to run fifth at the world championships.

The other disappointment for me was Steve Williams. Williams was, and still is, the only person to equal the world record in the 100 meters five times. In 1976 he appeared absolutely unbeatable. He ran against the very best in the country and easily won in record or near-record times. Everything was going well until the trial heats for the 100 meters. He was easily winning with a full head of steam, but then he eased up by leaning back before the tape. His leg swung forward hard, hyperextended, and caused damage to the muscle tissue behind the knee.

Because Williams ran so well in April and May and was hurt at the Olympic trials, it was commonly felt that he had burned out in the early races. As his coach, I took a lot of criticism for having him run too fast too soon. What people did not know was despite the fact that Williams had been winning regularly, he never purposely ran hard—just fast enough and hard enough to win. We had trained and planned along the very same lines as we had with McGrady. I wanted to get the competition out of the way early and be able to focus on making the team later.

Steve Williams and Robin Campbell were like my own children, so the disappointment at not having them make the team was even more painful because of our close relationship. The criticism and abuse directed at me was all the more frustrating because I was certain that we had done things right. By all odds they should have made the team, but it was not to be.

My trials in 1976, though, were not yet over. As assistant coach for the U.S. Women's Olympic Team, I was in charge of the 4 × 100 and 4 × 400 in Montreal. The sprinters I had for the 4 × 100 were Brenda Moorehead, Chandra Cheeseborough, Evelyn Ashford, and Debbie Armstrong. The first three were among the top seven sprinters at the Olympics, and the team was one of the favorites for the gold medal.

At that time, Brenda Moorehead was America's top female sprinter, with Cheeseborough and Ashford both ranked just behind her. Moorehead and Cheeseborough were teammates at Tennessee State University, coached by the famous Ed Temple, whose athletes have won more than thirty-five Olympic medals. No one else has come close to matching the number of Olympic gold medalists he has produced.

In putting together the 4 × 100, I asked Temple for his advice about the order of the team. He pointed out that on his relay team, Moorehead was the lead-off leg and Cheeseborough the anchor. This being the case, I decided to run Moorehead first, Ashford second, Armstrong third, and anchor Cheeseborough fourth. But what made perfect sense to Ed Temple at Tennessee State did not make sense to Brenda Moorehead at Montreal. As America's number one sprinter, Brenda probably felt that she should anchor.

There had also been bad blood between Moorehead and Ashford from the Pan American Games the previous summer. Ashford, not Moorehead, had anchored that team. I learned all of this later, but I should have suspected something at the time, as Moorehead just could not get the baton passed to Ashford. Moorehead would either run past Ashford, or she would not run fast enough to catch her.

During the training camp before the Olympic Games, the relay team became demoralized, Moorehead lost interest in the Olympic Games, and she also sustained an injury. The relay team finished a dismal fifth, with Martha Watson, a long jumper, running Moorehead's leg.

Again I received a great deal of criticism. I vowed not to forget the very hard lessons that 1976 had taught me.

I wondered if Ed Temple had had this kind of trouble when his team won the 4 × 100 in the 1960 Olympics. I wondered if I was wrong in asking his advice. No, I concluded, but it might have been better for him to be there to help sort out the trouble between his two athletes and Evelyn Ashford. The idea struck me that having the athlete's coaches on hand to sort out personality and ego conflicts was a great deal better than having a complete stranger trying to do it.

Eight years later, I had another chance, the chance of a lifetime. I was selected as the head women's coach for the 1984 U.S. Olympic Team. It was the perfect opportunity to redeem myself. The first thing I did was to lobby for maximum participation of the personal coaches of the athletes right up until the actual competition.

This was a radical departure from tradition. In the past, after the athletes had made the U.S. Olympic team, their personal coaches immediately became persona non grata. There are many instances in the past where the Olympic coaches took over completely. They made the personal coaches look on from outside the fence and did not permit them to have direct contact with their athletes.

This policy created strain and jealousy between the personal coaches and the Olympic coaches. The ones caught in the middle of this power struggle were the athletes themselves, and their performances suffered as a result.

Despite the obvious advantages of allowing personal coaches access to their athletes, it was not an easy idea to sell the powers that be. After all, it had never been done that way before. In addition, there were many proprietary interests which had to be protected, in particular, the idea that once the team was selected, it became the responsibility of the coaches, staff, and administrators selected to run the team.

We first tried involving the personal coaches at the world championship in 1983. There was a great deal of resistance to this innovation because it created more problems for the people who had to administer the team. But as the Athletics Congress was dedicated to doing whatever it took to make our 1984 Olympic team as successful as possible, they supported us. We chose to involve the personal coaches the most in the 4 × 100 race.

"You cannot run a relay team by committee," we had been warned, and the results at the world championships seemed to bear that out. Going into the mcet, the relay team had the second fastest time in the world, but the anchor dropped the baton, and the team did not qualify for the finals. The criticism was scalding, but it hardened my resolve even more.

I must admit that I had some doubts about whether my relay teams were ever going to show their stuff. I had the distinct feeling that I was somehow jinxing the runners on the relay teams. But I never wavered in my conviction that personal coaches needed to be with their athletes even, if possible, right up until the time they raced. It was and still is my feeling that whoever got the athletes this far would keep them there, and that the role of the Olympic coach was to facilitate and enhance the training that the personal coaches wanted.

I was fortunate to have a staff on the women's side that also accepted the concept. The head men's coach, Larry Ellis, was also supportive. Despite opposition, we were finally able to get key personal coaches to the training and warm-up venues in Los Angeles.

When we had encountered administrative problems, we moved practice to a site outside the Olympic village where the personal coaches could be with their athletes. We did not ask athletes to be in the Olympic village during the games despite strong objections by the U.S. Olympic Committee. The upshot was that we were successful in getting more personal coaches involved more deeply than ever before.

In the end, the U.S. Women's Olympic Team scored seven gold, seven silver, and two bronze medals. They also set six Olympic Games records. This was the greatest showing ever by a women's team in Olympic history. But for me, the most satisfying race was the 4 × 100 relay where Chandra Cheeseborough successfully passed the baton to her old rival Evelyn Ashford. Their relay team won the gold medal and set a new Olympic record.

What was the Winning Edge? Sometimes success is the result of having a good idea and being stubborn enough not to be swayed from it. Here, two athletes who seemed utterly incompatible eight years earlier teamed up to work in perfect harmony and reap the rewards in gold. But, even when you're doing what you know is right, there is no absolute guarantee of success. It's just not to be had. You still need luck.

Our Winning Edge was finding what was right and consistently applying it, even in the face of defeat, embarrassment, and criticism